Helping children with reading and spelling

This book provides teaching suggestions to help children who struggle with learning to read and spell. As a basic kit for class teachers, it collects in one place enough ideas to enable teachers and parents to give each child appropriate help. The teaching plans, including the 'five-minute-plan', have been written with the primary school child in mind, but can be modified for older pupils.

The materials build on the content of an earlier manual, Learning Difficulties in Reading and Writing, which has been widely and successfully used by teachers, especially those working with children who have specific literacy difficulties. The detailed teaching sequences, combining the enjoyment of content with the more systematic practice of sub-skills, which were particularly appreciated in the earlier volume, have been further developed here.

Helping Children with Reading and Spelling contains photocopiable materials and case examples. It is consistent with the English National Curriculum Programmes of Study and the Code of Practice on the Identification and Assessment of Special Educational Needs. Teachers using the manual will be following the school-based stages of intervention recommended by the Code and will be providing an invaluable basis for further action.

As plans to assist children with literacy difficulties are an integral part of the plans made for all the children in the classroom, two chapters contain examples illustrating arrangements which have incorporated help with reading and spelling into the daily class routine.

Rea Reason has worked as a primary and specialist teacher and as an educational psychologist in several local authorities. She now teaches in the School of Education, University of Manchester, and is co-author, with Peter Pumfrey, of Specific Learning Difficulties (Dyslexia) (Routledge 1992).

Rene Boote is an experienced primary and secondary teacher, and was formerly Head of the Reading and Language Support Service in Stockport LEA.

A SPECIAL NEEDS MANUAL

Helping children with reading and spelling

*Rea Reason
and Rene Boote*

RoutledgeFalmer
Taylor & Francis Group

LONDON AND NEW YORK

First published 1994
by Routledge
11 New Fetter Lane, London EC4P 4EE

Simultaneously published in the USA and Canada
by Routledge
a division of Routledge, Chapman and Hall, Inc.
29 West 35th Street, New York, NY 10001

Reprinted 1995 (twice), 1997, 1999

Reprinted 2001, 2002, 2003, 2004 by RoutledgeFalmer

RoutledgeFalmer is an imprint of the Taylor & Francis Group

© 1994 Rea Reason and Rene Boote

Typeset in Palatino, Sapir Sans and Jott by Tony Moss
Printed and bound in Great Britain by The Alden Group, Oxford

British Library Cataloguing in Publication Data
A catalogue record for this book is available from the British Library

Library of Congress Cataloguing in Publication Data
A catalogue record for this book is available from the Library of
Congress

ISBN 0-415-10733-4

Contents

Illustrations

Figures

Tables

PREFACE

This manual comes at a propitious time. The Dearing review of the national curriculum promises some degree of relief from the overwhelming demands of a nine subject curriculum and provides a much needed vote of confidence in teachers' judgements on what and how to teach. It also recognises that more must be done to ensure that the programmes of study are accessible at all levels.

As the Dearing review is implemented, teachers may find more time to work with children needing additional help with literacy. This manual contains suggestions on how the hard-pressed primary teacher can make the most effective use of even five minutes of extra assistance within a classroom that takes account of individual differences and needs.

Teachers should be able to turn to a member of staff with designated responsibilities for children with special needs - sometimes known as special educational needs co-ordinators (SENCOs). Every primary school is being asked to ensure that at least one teacher has the knowledge, skills and opportunities to work with colleagues in identifying pupils with difficulties and developing strategies for helping them. The 1993 Education Act and the **Code of Practice** make it mandatory for every school to have a policy on the identification and assessment of pupils with special educatonal needs. Early identification and intervention are essential to good special needs provision.

The Centre for Educational Needs at Manchester University has been working intensively with teachers to ensure means of access to the 'broad, balanced and relevant curriculum' to which all children are legally entitled. It has developed materials to support teachers in helping pupils with severe and complex learning difficulties gain access to the national curriculum and to benefit from the curriculum as a whole. In addition, Trevor Payne has instigated work with teachers of pupils with specific or moderate learning difficulties and collected examples of practice when the national curriculum was first introduced.

The present manual builds on these earlier initiatives. It provides a wealth of practical ideas for teachers wishing to help pupils with special needs in the areas of reading and spelling. It is based on much experience in the classroom and on many years of working with teachers in workshops and courses. It is rooted in our growing understanding of the foundations of literacy and the difficulties which some children experience with the learning processes involved.

Professor Peter Mittler
University of Manchester

ACKNOWLEDGEMENTS

Among the many friends and colleagues who have contributed their experience and support to the writing of this book, we wish especially to thank Christine Proctor, Helen Moss and Bronach Bansal for their case examples and suggestions, and Eleri Batowski, Rachel Gallagher and Sarah Boote for their comments on the completed manuscript. We are also indebted to Muriel Bridge and Angela White for allowing us to adapt materials originally devised by them. The picture illustrations were drawn by Pat Williams who combined her expertise as a special needs teacher with her artistic talents. We are particularly grateful to Tony Moss whose desktop publishing skills proved invaluable in preparing the manuscript for publication.

We would not have embarked on the task of writing this manual without the encouragement provided by members of the Centre for Educational Needs at Manchester University, in particular Peter Mittler, Peter Pumfrey, Gina Conti-Ramsden and Peter Farrell. Special thanks go to Trevor Payne whose previous work in the Centre influenced our thinking about the implications of the National Curriculum for pupils with special needs in literacy. We were also much assisted by the comments of the 1992-94 cohort of students undertaking the Advanced Diploma in Specific Learning Difficulties at the Centre. Most of all we were helped by the many pupils, parents and teachers in schools who have followed our suggestions and found them useful.

USE OF COPYRIGHT MATERIAL

Part 1

Main Themes
and Ideas

Chapter 1

AN OVERVIEW OF THE MANUAL

This chapter describes the purposes, main themes and rationale of the manual. We regard it as essential reading before progressing to the other chapters which focus in more detail on particular teaching plans.

THE PURPOSE OF THE MANUAL

This manual consists of teaching plans to help children who struggle with learning to read, write and spell. It is intended as a basic kit for class teachers and collects in one place enough ideas to enable teachers and parents to give each child appropriate help. The teaching suggestions have been written with the primary school child in mind, but can be modified for older pupils.

At the same time, the manual does not set out to be an exhaustive account of teaching methods for pupils with special needs in reading and spelling; nor a substitute for more extensive help. When a child has followed the programmes outlined in this manual for a period of time and continues to have marked and persistent difficulties, your school's special needs policy will guide you in what you do next. Your systematic records of the way in which you are helping the child will provide an invaluable basis for further action.

Evaluations of our previous manual showed that teachers and parents appreciated the framework which combined shared activities, focusing on the enjoyment of content, with the more systematic practice of subskills. The detailed teaching sequences were particularly valued. Follow-up studies demonstrated that pupils with difficulties had made good progress when their teaching was based on the methods presented in the manual (Reason, 1986).

The manual began as a collection of practical ideas drawn from our own experiences as teachers of pupils with special needs in literacy. To these were added suggestions made by colleagues and the many teachers who participated in the courses that we ran. The ideas were consistent with our knowledge of research and theory about the development of literacy.

This new manual includes the following improvements:

- Teaching suggestions have been extended and amplified to take account of current developments.

- Tables and figures make it easier to locate particular items in order to plan a comprehensive programme.

- Clearer links are made between assessment and teaching sequences.

- Up-to-date case examples illustrate specific methods and the overall approach.

- The manual is based on relevant educational legislation in the areas of special needs and the teaching of English.

Learning to read and write integrates many experiences and skills. The language curriculum must proceed on a broad front. But in a manual of this kind, information cannot be presented in other than a linear and sequential way. To overcome the limitations imposed by any book format, we present our rationale for teaching literacy in this chapter. This takes three forms:

- Figure 1.1 illustrates our model of how aspects of literacy learning interact and overlap. It is introduced in this chapter and subsequent chapters focus on different areas of the diagram.

- Figure 1.2 shows the educational context in which individual planning and instruction takes place.

- A question and answer section clarifies the themes and assumptions that recur throughout the manual.

A MODEL OF LITERACY LEARNING

Figure 1.1 illustrates the complementary and overlapping nature of reading and writing. The three central areas distinguish between **meaning, phonics** and **fluency** in the following way:

- **Meaning** covers the understanding and enjoyment of content.

- **Phonics** refers to phonological competencies and the teaching of word analysis skills.

- **Fluency** is effortless and automatic word recognition and reproduction.

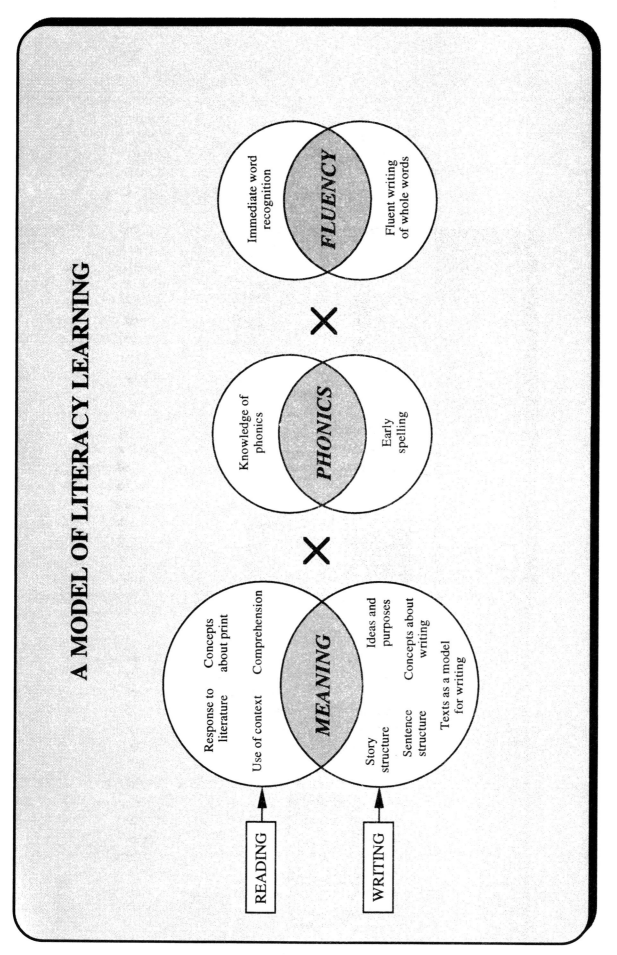

A MODEL OF LITERACY LEARNING

FLUENCY
Immediate word recognition
Fluent writing of whole words

PHONICS
Knowledge of phonics
Early spelling

MEANING
Concepts about print
Comprehension
Response to literature
Use of context
Ideas and purposes
Concepts about writing
Story structure
Sentence structure
Texts as a model for writing

READING

WRITING

Figure. 1.1   © Reason and Boote, 1994. This page may be reproduced without infringing copyright.

It is no accident that the circles relating to **meaning** are the largest in the diagram. There would be no point in pursuing the other two areas if the foundations of communication had not been developed and maintained. The importance of sharing books and other written information with children cannot easily be exaggerated.

But the various skills and competencies associated with **phonics** and **fluency** may not occur simply through a familiarity with the content of books. Some children need to have the connections between literary content and the way it is written down made very explicit. They need to practise skills out of context as necessary, and to observe the practical applications of the same skills in other literary contexts.

The English National Curriculum programmes of study in **Speaking and Listening** are essential for literacy learning and particularly important for the development of the **meaning** areas in the figure. Although these oral and auditory areas are not directly represented, we assume that you are familiar with relevant Speaking and Listening activities. Those emphasising discussion and shared learning are of particular importance.

Figure 1.1 illustrates three important points:

1. The three areas of **meaning, phonics** and **fluency** are not merely added together: they have a *multiplying* effect on each other. Knowledge in one area interacts with and supports knowledge in the other areas, making subsequent learning easier. We assume that the reader learns to synthesize simultaneously information from several sources: previous experience, knowledge of meaning and grammar, and visual and phonic information. When there is difficulty with one source of information, another may compensate for it. It is possible, for example, to deduce the meaning of a word from its context and the context can also sometimes make up for problems with word recognition. In fluent reading, word recognition skills have become much more automatic, and use of context is likely to remain central to the comprehension of what is read.

2. Reading and writing instruction is not confined to any single approach. To select 'real reading' or 'phonics' or 'look and say' as an exclusive teaching method would deny children a full opportunity to develop all the necessary concepts and skills. In the same way, to concentrate on spelling at the expense of creativity, or creative writing without instruction in spelling and handwriting leads to imbalance, and failure to acquire important skills. A similar imbalance would result from selecting any other aspect as an exclusive approach.

3. Reading and writing complement and support each other, but need a different emphasis when taught to ensure that children can apply necessary skills. Teaching children strategies for reading will not automatically mean that they can adapt the same strategies to writing, and vice versa. For example,

in reading it is possible to guess unknown words from context whereas in accurate spelling there is little scope for approximations. On the other hand, early spelling development does usually lead to an appreciation of phonological regularities which develops reading.

Our model of literacy is not intended to be revolutionary or exceptional. It represents the views of the many teachers who have discussed their work with us. A quotation from an extensive review of the effects of different kinds of tutoring programmes illustrates our practical research basis:

> ...*programmes with the most comprehensive models of reading, and therefore the most complete instructional interventions, appear to have larger impacts than programmes which address only a few components of the reading process.*
> *(Wasik and Slavin 1993, p 196)*

Implications for the manual:

- **The three areas of meaning, phonics and fluency provide the basic framework for assessment and teaching.**

- **Reading and writing activities are planned in a way which enables them to complement each other.**

- **Different chapters focus on particular areas of the diagram and describe in detail the teaching methods involved.**

THE BROADER EDUCATIONAL CONTEXT

We recognise that plans to assist children with literacy difficulties are an integral part of the plans made for all the children in the classroom. Overall school policies and practices determine how the needs of the individual are being met. **Figure 1.2** illustrates the educational philosophy of the manual. Although the manual will focus on detailed assessment and teaching strategies, other crucial areas determine the success of that instruction.

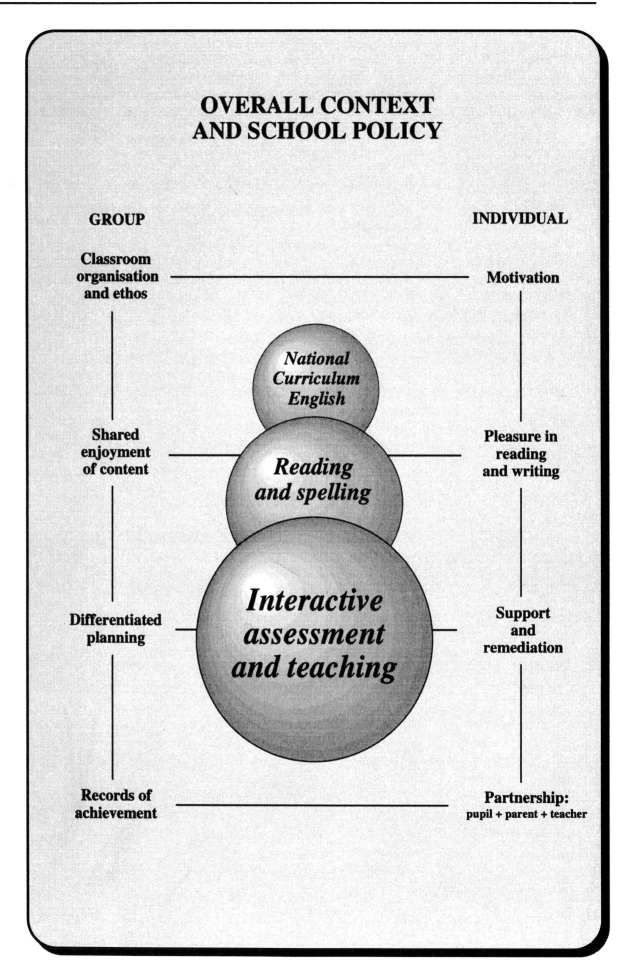

Figure 1.2   © Reason and Boote, 1994. This page may be reproduced without infringing copyright.

The centre of the diagram emphasises that knowledge of children's literacy learning and, in particular, those aspects relevant to difficulties with reading and spelling inform our approaches to interactive assessment and teaching. The third circle, National Curriculum English, provides the context for the decisions that need to be made.

These three areas cannot exist in isolation. They depend on the way teachers organise their classrooms and promote successful and enjoyable learning. The connecting lines between the headings for the group and for the individual illustrate their interdependence. For example, individual motivation is influenced by a general classroom ethos which enhances cooperation and supportive attitudes. Motivation is also dependent on a sense of success and pleasure in reading and writing which, in turn, is influenced by the way the whole class shares and enjoys the content of written information. And the way the whole class shares the enjoyment of content is again a function of classroom organisation and ethos.

Similarly, the two headings of 'differentiated planning' and 'support and remediation' are presented as complementary mirror images. Plans for the whole class take account of individual differences. Additional planning for the child with literacy difficulties then facilitates access to content, despite the difficulties, and provides specific help with learning to read and write.

At the bottom of the diagram, records of achievement for the whole class are juxtaposed with the partnership required from the pupil, parent and teacher when there are additional difficulties. Both sides have as their pre-requisites constructive self-assessments, the setting of attainable targets and the celebration of targets achieved.

Figure 1.2 is an overview of some of the most important issues in educational practice. Chapters 10 and 11 in the last part of this manual provide examples of its application within the overall classroom context.

> **Figure 1.2 underpins all the chapters in the manual.**
>
> **It stresses the importance of:**
>
> - **the overall educational context**
> - **positive feelings**
> - **constructive records**
> - **children's involvement in their own learning**
> - **an ethos of partnership**

SOME KEY QUESTIONS

Is the teaching of reading and spelling difficult?

A manual with many explanations, instructions and diagrams might imply that the teaching of reading and writing is an exceedingly complicated business. We wish to stress that this is not the case. For us, the 'feel good' factor is the most important ingredient of success. If we keep up the momentum of enjoyment and continue to provide opportunities for reading and writing in whatever form, then the teaching will combine with maturation to achieve sustained progress.

We believe that those planning a programme for children with literacy difficulties will find the information presented in this manual helpful, bearing in mind that our teaching methods are not offered as infallible prescriptions, but as suggestions which have proved successful with many children in the past.   There is no guarantee that they will work with all children in all situations. Whilst theoretical knowledge of the learning processes involved in reading and writing remain incomplete, it is essential to keep an open mind rather than subscribe rigidly to any one method. It is important, however, to adopt a systematic approach in planning for the individual child with difficulties.

How can I find the time for the individual work?

We are well aware of the considerable pressures on teacher time. We have been encouraged, however, by comments such as: 'Knowing what to do makes it easier to find the time for doing it'. Many teachers have also said that having a clearer idea of the child's progress and literacy needs makes it possible to incorporate some of the activities into the daily class routine. Isolated help outside the classroom cannot achieve that kind of transfer into other aspects of the school work.

How, then, can the busy class teacher find time to follow the suggestions made in this manual? Teachers have attempted to solve the problem in a number of ways. In some schools, overall policy has favoured opportunities for individual work so that arrangements have been made to free each class teacher in turn to work individually with some children.   With regard to overall classroom organisation, teachers have found the approaches outlined in Chapter 11 useful in helping children to work together, so giving the teacher more time to focus on particular aspects. Sometimes several children in the class may require similar additional help, and be taught together as a group. Chapter 10 provides an illustration of this way of working.

We recognise, however, that most class teachers have very limited time for individual instruction. The 'five-minute-plan' below requires more than five minutes at the initial assessment and planning stages. After that, however, the daily 'five minutes' of systematic help, together with other appropriate classroom activities, can result in very pleasing progress.

A FIVE-MINUTE-PLAN

- If you can give the child with difficulties a maximum of five minutes of individual attention per day, you need to decide about the child's priorities.

- Consider first what you would do in an ideal situation with plenty of time. This manual helps you design an initial plan.

- Now decide what is possible and what compromises you have to make.

- As you focus on particular activities, keep in mind the areas that are not being covered so that you may correct the balance later.

- Examples of initial plans are provided at the end of Chapter 3, page 49

How do I define Specific Learning Difficulties (Dyslexia)?

This is indeed a highly controversial question as different researchers and practitioners tend to define Specific Learning Difficulties in different ways. These issues have been considered in many publications (e.g. Pumfrey and Reason, 1991). In our experience, Specific Learning Difficulties range from mild to severe. The use of the label then depends on rather arbitrary cut-off points along a continuum of difficulties.

In this manual, we define Specific Learning Difficulties as marked and persistent lack of progress with the printed word. With reference to **Figure 1.1**, it means that the child's progress in the areas of **Phonics** and **Fluency** has not kept pace with the progress that he or she has made within the **Meaning** areas of the diagram. Such difficulties have been linked with problems with phonological awareness and processing. For this reason, Chapter 3 of the manual contains initial assessments of the phonological competencies of children and subsequent chapters describe in detail appropriate methods of teaching.

The children causing concern tend to have much difficulty in starting to learn to read and write independently. A few seem unable to make a start at all despite being experts at 'reading the pictures' and generally enjoying the content of books and other written information. Older pupils can often make extensive use of contextual and language cues without sufficient back-up from knowledge of sound/symbol correspondences. For example, 'house' may be read as 'home' or 'trees' may be read as 'wood'. These kinds of errors can be made by any of us when reading fast. But it is the frequency of the errors combined with a relatively slow and halting reading style that distinguishes older children with specific difficulties.

At the same time, the spelling of the older pupils can be so unconventional that even they themselves cannot decipher what they have written on an earlier occasion. And, to make matters worse, many are struggling with the task of making their handwriting legible.

The extent and nature of the difficulties vary, and no two children have the same pattern of problems. Where children with such difficulties appear to be quite like their friends in most other respects, teachers and parents may look for causes, whether constitutional or environmental, to explain the discrepancy. Children are described as dyslexic or as having deficient auditory or visual perception or memory. Often difficulties with rote learning, such as memorising multiplication tables, are cited as evidence for specific memory defects. These aspects may be of theoretical importance. Parents may derive comfort from the thought that no one is to blame and that their child is not stupid or lazy. But labels such as 'dyslexia' or 'specific difficulties' do not in themselves help the teacher or the parent to decide what or how to teach.

The term Specific Learning Difficulties has the advantage of reminding us to look at children's performance in the learning situation, to specify what the children can and cannot do with regard to the tasks of reading and writing, and to set appropriate learning targets which relate directly to the reading and writing. In this way teaching can be planned for every child regardless of labels. A few will progress very slowly despite the systematic help. They have been identified, through their response to teaching, as having more serious difficulties and as requiring more extensive individual help. In identifying these children we need to remember the following principles:

- Any child, regardless of ability or socio-cultural background, can experience specific difficulties with the print aspects of literacy.

- Emotional factors may play a part, but this becomes a 'chicken and egg' situation in that failure to progress with reading and writing has itself emotional repercussions.

- Reading and writing difficulties can range from mild to severe. Every primary school class will have some children who are not learning to read and spell as easily as the majority. All these children need to be helped and most will progress as a result of good teaching and maturation. A few will need more extensive additional help.

- The term 'developmental delay' has been used to explain these difficulties. The term has important practical implications. If the child has not been able to take full advantage of the learning opportunities provided at the age of five, he or she will be able to do so at the age of six or seven or later. It is essential, therefore, that the missed opportunities at the earlier age are compensated for later through at least equally intensive and skilled teaching.

What about bilingual children?

Cultural and linguistic diversity enriches society. Being able to speak many languages is a great asset. In the world as a whole, monolingual speakers are in the minority. In the United Kingdom, however, the term 'the bilingual child' usually denotes children from minority ethnic communities who are considered to be at a disadvantage because their mother tongue is not English. In British schools the children rarely have the opportunity to become literate in their first language before learning a second language. In many cases, children are learning to understand and speak a new language, namely English, at the same time as they start to learn to read and write in that language.

In order to appreciate and take advantage of the children's own cultural backgrounds, what do we need to know as teachers? What should we do to help children maintain their first language and build on their existing linguistic competencies when learning the second language? These issues are discussed in many publications. We particularly recommend the resource materials entitled Bilingual Pupils and the National Curriculum (Cline and Frederickson, 1991) which consider learning difficulties within the context of promoting a multicultural and multilingual society.

In this manual our concern is primarily with difficulties in learning about the print aspects of literacy. We start by ensuring that children enjoy and understand the content as it is essential to take advantage of these content cues when learning the written 'code'. If children cannot understand the content and also struggle with deciphering the print, they have a double disadvantage.

Even when children speak English, they will comprehend the content according to their own cultural 'scripts'. Take for example the following text quoted by Wallace (1986):

> Sally's daddy said we are going to see Auntie Pat in hospital.
> Sally and her daddy went to a shop to get some...
> (From Link-Up: Auntie Pat in Hospital)

Predicting that the word 'flowers' follows will not be obvious to those children for whom flower buying is not part of the 'script' for visiting people in hospital. The example demonstrates the difficulty of learning about print through familiar texts if the texts are not relevant to the children's own life experiences.

The promotion of equal opportunities supports those approaches which emphasise reciprocity and the validity of all experiences, perspectives and cultures. Where children have to learn a new spoken language and literacy simultaneously, teaching methods usually focus on the meaning aspects of Figure1.1. The purpose of communication is paramount.

But some children, regardless of background, will also need to learn about phonology and word recognition in a more systematic way. Their specific learning difficulties may be masked by their limited mastery of the English language. What is needed then is not one approach but an assessment of the most suitable combination of methods required by the individual. This is achieved through observations of how the child responds to the teaching.

HOW TO USE THE MANUAL

The teaching suggestions in this manual are not, in essence, different from those recommended for all children. They differ only in being more deliberate and more detailed. Given enough time, you can use the manual to plan individual learning programmes similar to those advocated by Marie Clay (1991).

Start by tracing back and checking that earlier stages of learning have been accomplished. Tables of reading and spelling development in Chapter 3 and Chapter 8 respectively are designed to help you to do this. Your observations lead to a programme which includes the three elements of **meaning, phonics** and **fluency** illustrated in Figure 1.1 on page 5 and involves:

- **Reading and writing together (Chapter 2)**

- **Increased repetition to enhance fluency (Chapters 4 and 5)**

- **Systematic teaching of phonological awareness and phonics (Chapters 6 and 7)**

- **Help with spelling and handwriting (Chapters 8 and 9)**

Given less time, you can design a five-minute-plan as described on page 11. It still involves initial observations drawing on **Chapter 3** for reading and **Chapter 8** for spelling. But you then consider priorities on the basis of the time and resources available to you.

Chapters 10 and 11 provide examples of work undertaken in mainstream primary classrooms. They demonstrate arrangements which have succeeded in incorporating help with reading and spelling into the daily class routine.

Chapter 2

MEANING AND MOTIVATION

This chapter discusses teaching methods. We consider the emotional consequences of learning difficulties and provide examples of the way children, parents and teachers can work together.

THE IMPORTANCE OF MEANING

Teachers and parents try to make sure that first experiences of reading and writing are purposeful and pleasurable for all children. This may not prevent some children from finding it difficult to read and write independently for themselves. But whatever drills and skills-learning we judge to be necessary for their progress, we must remember that reading and writing are concerned with receiving and transmitting meaning.

We have met children who could read and spell with unusual accuracy, but who did it only at the direction of the teacher, and hardly ever for their own purposes. They were not making full use of the power of literacy to convey meaning. We have also met children who read with great enthusiasm but little accuracy, sometimes completely misinterpreting the text, and those whose spelling makes their writing incomprehensible, even to themselves. These children were neither receiving nor transmitting the correct meaning. In either case the purpose of learning to read and spell had disappeared from view.

THEORIES OF INSTRUCTION

Over the years, two opposing theories of how children best learn to read and write have emerged; and they have each attracted strong support from teachers, parents, researchers, and the general public. At one extreme stand the proponents of 'whole language', 'real' books, and learning to read and write simply by reading and writing. This has been labelled the 'top-down' approach. In contrast, those who advocate the 'bottom-up' approach believe that complex skills need to be built up from their elements, and that children learn to read and write more effectively by controlled practice of letter sounds and word recognition, or 'good old-fashioned phonics and spelling'.

'Top-down' starts from shared interest, gentle assistance and ample opportunity to learn through the enjoyment of content. Children learn to recognise printed words by associating them first with their existing knowledge about spoken language and with their general experience. In contrast, the 'bottom-up' way of teaching assumes that word recognition skills should be learnt first through structured cumulative methods of teaching individual words and letter-sounds.

The polarisation of these two viewpoints has resulted in heated debate. Teachers, faced with children who struggle to learn reading and spelling, believe that it is not a question of one approach to the exclusion of the other. They want to know how to combine the most suitable elements of both. How can understanding of content develop if one starts from word recognition, or word recognition result from enjoyment of content?

Ways of blending the two have been considered in previous publications (Reason, 1990; Pumfrey and Reason,1991). Figure 2.1, an upturned triangle, is taken from that work. The starting point is the overall context of learning and its meaning for the child. Children need ample opportunity to experience the way spoken language is represented in print, so that they may predict the text in reading, and make reasonable guesses in spelling. The implications for teaching are that reading and writing can profitably be taught together, as outlined later in this chapter.

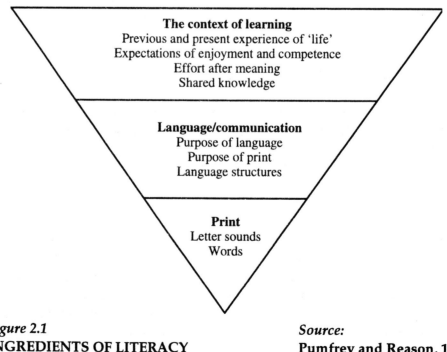

Figure 2.1
INGREDIENTS OF LITERACY

Source:
Pumfrey and Reason, 1991

The reader's previous experiences will determine whether the thoughts expressed by the writers can make sense to them. Their own 'experiences of life' provide the basis for the choice of materials, and it is particularly important to ensure that cultural and linguistic diversity is taken into account here.

Expectations of enjoyment and competence are the next key factor. Observations indicate that children making slow progress in literacy read much less than those making good progress. The emotional effects of learning difficulties can lead to lower initial expectations of success, giving up more easily, and tending to attribute success to luck, and failure to one's own lack of competence. Learning is adversely affected by worry and anxiety.

These observations demonstrate the cumulative effects of early difficulties. Some children increasingly avoid reading and writing, becoming demotivated and unwilling to learn. The resultant lack of opportunity to develop underlying competencies can then contribute to the children's difficulties. Such children may not have severe and intractable literacy difficulties, but simply have 'missed the boat' at an earlier age. For any number of reasons, they may not have been quite ready to take the opportunity to learn at Infant age when the other children were learning. Those opportunities were not repeated later. In any case, motivation to take advantage of them might have vanished by then. The strength of the kind of reading recovery programme introduced by Clay (1979) is that children's difficulties are noticed at an early age.

Learning to deal with the grapho-phonic (letter-sound) aspects of print in literacy is the last, but nonetheless essential, element. It is dependent on the other major areas of language described above. A few children have considerable difficulties with this small but vital area and do require carefully planned extra help. For them too, 'top-down' approaches, which focus on meaning, provide the continued foundations for additional 'bottom-up' instruction of aspects such as phonics.

THE CONCEPT OF APPRENTICESHIP

The phrase 'the apprenticeship approach' has been the source of much debate and distortion. One misinterpretation of the term leads to the assumption that children will just 'catch' reading if they have enough 'good books' read to them. The instructional support provided by reading schemes may have been too readily and too categorically rejected.

If the metaphor of 'apprenticeship' is referred back to its origin, we are reminded that those who wished to master a craft such as cabinet-making or weaving learnt partly by watching the expert at work, and taking note of his explanations and comments, partly by rehearsing isolated skills, and partly by supervised practice. Motivation for sustained effort was provided by the satisfaction of doing small things well, and by constant access to practical examples of finished articles. Learning to read and spell can be successfully approached in a similar way, if we remember that children's main access to the 'finished article' is by having books read to them. But this access is not sufficient in itself to enable skills practice to be dispensed with.

In our experience, teachers do not have the time to devise their own 'apprentice approach' from scratch, and like to have the organisational back-up provided by reading schemes. The cumulative structure of the schemes helps busy teachers to plan for individual children. 'An A to Z of Reading Schemes' published by NASEN and updated at regular intervals, lists and describes current schemes according to their reading and interest levels (see Addresses, page 198 of the manual). The list is particularly valuable in helping teachers to choose easier books with an interest level to appeal to older children.

Many recently published schemes contain books and other material which are well presented, interesting and fun to read. In contrast, some non-scheme books may be boring or irrelevant to a particular child. Now that reading scheme books are designed to be enjoyed as well as to instruct, the division between books that children like to read and books that children learn to read with seems artificial and unnecessary. Reading schemes provide a convenient 'spine' for the reading curriculum. Other stories, information books, rhymes, poems, songs, riddles, comics and books created by the children themselves provide the broader experience of reading. What we offer children to read influences whether they enjoy reading, but the way we help them to read enables them to a greater or lesser degree to read independently. This is why the interpretation given to 'the apprentice approach' is important.

Coles (1992) provides a clear and readable account of three overlapping phases of learning through apprenticeship. These are: observation, coaching and practice. In summarising his work, we have adapted suggestions to include both reading and writing.

Observation

The teacher's task is to model reading and writing while the child listens to the content or dictates the content. This includes incidental reference to the vocabulary involved as described in Vocabulary of Reading on page 34. For example:

> *Here is the front of the book. This is where the title is and it says.... Now, let me start reading - I'll start from the top of the page here ...*

Similarly for writing:

> *What's the name of your story? I'll write it here. Now I'm writing the first word ... Let me read to you what you told me. I like it. I like it because...What shall we write now? I'll start with the first letter ...*

When reading to the child teachers make their own strategies more explicit through skillful intonation and commentary. For example:

"I wonder what will happen next?" "I think that .... will happen next because..." "What do you think will happen?" (Teachers may sometimes make 'silly' predictions and let the child correct them.)

At the early stages of literacy, activities will include many nursery rhymes, action rhymes and word games. Books such as The Mouse in the House (by Henrietta and published by Dorling Kindersley) will enable children to develop their phonological awareness while attending to the interesting pictures and content. There is no artificial divide between meaning and starting to learn about phonics.

Coaching

The teacher and child read together. The child might 'hear' the teacher read by pointing to the words. Or the teacher reads most of the text and lets the child have a go where she feels certain the child can succeed. They stop occasionally to have a reading conversation which draws out key areas of the content. Gradually, through the re-reading of familiar texts the child takes over. A similar sequence can be followed in writing where the child starts by dictating content and gradually takes over some of the writing herself. The teacher offers the child a range of strategies for working out unknown words such as:

- pointing out the letter sounds that the child has learnt;

- making inferences from context and the letter sounds when reading;

- showing how long words can be broken up into smaller chunks.

Practice

As children become more competent they move into the phase of independent practice. Their strategies are increasingly internalised and, depending on the materials, they progress because they want to read and write. And the more they read and write the better they become at it. The teacher's task is now to:

- promote and encourage private reading;

- help children to 'share' the books they have enjoyed through classroom activities involving talking about the content; book reports; and, if possible, provision of several copies of favourite books;

- help children to become 'writing partners' or 'response friends' by learning to work together.

IMPLICATIONS FOR CHILDREN WITH LITERACY DIFFICULTIES

In the apprenticeship approach there is an easy overlap between the three aspects of **meaning, fluency** and **phonics** where particular points are noted and discussed within the context of reading or writing together. In deciding on the points to be noted the teacher needs to be sensitive to the child's progress and have enough background knowledge to judge when prompts are necessary. If there are too many prompts, the child remains dependent on the teacher and does not start to move into the independent phase. If there are too few, the child becomes discouraged and progress is hampered.

What can we do about those children who do not start to attend to phonological aspects at the **observation** phase or who are 'stuck' at the **coaching** phase? They may love books and have plenty to say when dictating their own content, but continue to be reliant on the teacher or parent to read and write for them. The important foundations of meaning and communication have been achieved. Aspects of **fluency** and **phonics** require more deliberate attention as described in the relevant chapters of this manual.

But the success and interest achieved in the **meaning** area must be maintained. When learning the mechanics of reading and writing is hard work, then it is particularly important that the child also has opportunities just to relax and enjoy the content. We need to read to the children material of their choice and act as their scribes when they are unable to record something themselves. We also need to take account of the emotional and motivational consequences of literacy difficulties as described below.

MOTIVATION

Nothing succeeds like success. Pupils who make good progress take pride in their efforts. Their confidence in being able to complete a task brings them half-way towards doing so. But even when the school does not emphasise competition, they measure their achievements against the performance of the other children in the class and they may be judged by their peers and also by their teachers in terms of how well they keep up with their classmates. The 'pecking order' is there whether we like it or not, and is being further emphasised by national curriculum testing.

Children who feel successful develop a positive self-image at school which is further reinforced at home when parents are pleased with their progress. The situation for children with learning difficulties can be the opposite. They may approach the learning task believing that they will not be able to complete it and their lack of confidence causes their performance to deteriorate even further. They become reluctant to try, they prevaricate, daydream and appear to be making little effort to learn. In the classroom they may concentrate their efforts on remaining inconspicuous whilst at the same time feeling guilty and inadequate.

In time such children may rationalize their disappointment by doing their best to convince themselves and others that they do not care about educational achievement. They may cultivate an attitude of indifference or, seeking the limelight at any cost, they may become classroom clowns or develop behaviour problems. Their concentration span is often limited because of the difficulty of the learning task and their distaste for it. At home they are likely to meet with disappointment and anxiety. The continuing lack of success at school may gradually generalize to other aspects of their personalities so that they increasingly regard themselves as inferior.

Fortunately, because of the remarkable resilience of most children, the very bleak picture we have outlined above rarely continues for long. Pupils can often compensate for their scholastic problems by succeeding in other areas at school and at home, and social acceptability in the playground is not usually dependent on educational achievements. But some elements of our description can be recognized in every pupil with learning difficulties, whether those difficulties are limited to literacy only, or whether they are of a more general nature.

At this point we need to examine our own feelings as teachers towards children with learning difficulties. We also take pride in success; seeing children learn and enjoy learning is proof of our success. When pupils are not responding to our efforts, we naturally feel disappointed, and their poor progress may threaten our sense of expertise as teachers. We can unwittingly convey our disappointment to the child and so make matters worse. Or we may seek explanations in terms of constitutional or environmental factors which label the child but which offer no constructive suggestions of what we can do to help.

Learning difficulties, particularly in literacy, cause parents very great anxiety. As parents we may see our child's failure as our own failure too. We want to help but we may feel inadequate to do so. And when we try to help, our child may avoid our help in the same way as they have learnt to avoid reading and writing at school, forgetting books or losing messages. We know that in order to help our child we need to remain encouraging and positive, but this can be very hard because we care so much. We may reveal our concern to our child even when we are trying to remain calm. For example, Sharon was avoiding reading with her father despite his willing offers. After much embarrassed silence she gave the following explanation: 'It would be all right if my dad didn't sigh all the time as he reads with me!'

PARENTS AS PARTNERS

The first action we can take is to form a team which involves the parent, the pupil and the teacher. The best starting point is an agreement by all that there is a difficulty, that nobody is to blame for the difficulty and that we can make the best progress by working together as a team. Parents and children will need to have a very clear idea of what to do at home, how to do it and how to record the progress made. It is important that a sense of mutual appreciation and trust is developed between all involved. This does not happen overnight. It will always require a great deal more contact between parents and teachers than they are used to. Regular meetings make heavy demands on time for both parents and teachers. Because the teamwork is central to the child's progress, we believe the time is well spent.

Some parents may have good reasons for not wanting to participate in teaching. They may feel that they are unable to remain calm and encouraging when helping their own children. This can be a familiar experience for teachers too, who have enormous patience when helping other people's children but are on a 'short fuse' when teaching their own. This is only natural. Our concern for our own children is so great that we become too involved in their difficulties. If we realize that our feelings of irritation and frustration are the consequences of that concern, and if the learning tasks are designed to promote rather than thwart a sense of achievement, then most parents are able to play a vital role in the teaching process.

It is clear that pupils will need a great deal of encouragement. Areas in which they are succeeding need to be noticed and appreciated. When learning is difficult, it may help to blame the task itself, for example the word that will not allow itself to be remembered, in order to alleviate feelings of inadequacy or guilt. We also need to recognise that learning the mechanics of reading and writing can be very hard work and require intense concentration which can only be sustained for a relatively short period of time.

Approaches which emphasise counselling to improve self-esteem can be of help. These are reviewed in Pumfrey and Reason (1991). We also need to stress the central role of a positive classroom atmosphere where children co-operate rather than compete. This is an essential aspect of Figure 1.2 in Chapter 1 and will be illustrated further in Chapter 11. But in our opinion the single most important contribution to a sense of success is to complete a task successfully. We may have to blinker ourselves to all the things the child should have learnt in order to keep up with his or her peers. We need to examine the task, in our case the reading and writing task, to assess what the pupil does know so that we can plan next steps of learning in a way that will ensure their successful completion.

PARENTS AS TEACHERS

Usually, on reaching school, the child will have acquired the language and understanding needed to begin to learn to read and write. If nursery rhymes, songs and stories have been read in the security of the home, these activities will have prepared the child for learning at school. The parents of the child with literacy difficulties will often have done the important ground work. The child enjoys stories and talks with interest and understanding about them. Although the development of independent reading and writing may prove to be very hard work, the child's knowledge of language can become invaluable in compensating for difficulties.

It is particularly important that parents continue to read aloud stories and information that the child wants to hear. This will keep the interest in content alive, and provide a continuing model of 'how reading works'. It will also maintain and develop the child's knowledge so that it is possible to keep up with those who have had the fortune to learn to read more easily.

As teaching is planned for the pupil along the lines described in this manual, teachers will find that many of the suggestions can be adapted for practice at home. Those approaches where parents read with their children for meaning and enjoyment, or act as scribes in order to help their children communicate their ideas are particularly valuable. All concerned need to feel that they have control over what is happening and that they are being fully consulted. If any of the communication links between the pupil, the teacher and the parent are faulty, motivation to learn and to teach will be affected.

The apprenticeship approach, described above, may contrast with the parents' expectations of 'hearing' children read. We need to stress the purpose of enjoying the content together rather than collecting books as 'trophies' that have been laboriously acquired, page by page, with little appreciation of the story as a whole. The principles of gentle coaching need to be emphasised. There can be much merit in re-reading favourite books.

PAIRED OR SHARED READING

The terms 'paired reading' and 'shared reading' have been used synonymously but in fact describe different approaches. Both have in common methods which consist of the parent and the child reading together from a book of the child's choice.

The term 'shared' relates to a range of activities appropriate for younger children. It links closely with the phases of **observation** and **coaching** described earlier in this chapter. Shared reading can be seen as a transitional stage between hearing a story read aloud and becoming an independent reader. The parent talks about the book, provides a model of reading and encourages the child to join in whenever possible. The child is actively involved and learns about the intonation and rhythms of reading.

A publication entitled *Shared Reading and Shared Writing* by the Centre for Language in Primary Education (1990) illustrates how these kinds of shared activities become the mainstay of literacy learning in the Infant classroom. They involve the use of Big Books where the text is enlarged so that the whole class can see it, read and re-read it, and discuss it. These activities are linked with shared writing, where the teacher and children write words or sentences from the book on large sheets of paper and, again, talk about them, re-read them and note particular instructional points such as rhyming words or identical initial letter sounds. In this way reading and writing activities complement each other.

Paired reading, on the other hand, describes a specific method where the child and the parent, or other more competent reader, read 'in chorus' together. The parent adjusts the pace of reading to suit the child. It involves two sets of instructions. In the first, entitled **reading together,** the parent and the child read each word aloud together. They usually read quite slowly. If the child struggles and hesitates for more than five seconds with a particular word, the parent says the word and the child repeats it after the parent. Reading in chorus then continues.

The second set of instructions, entitled **reading alone,** is followed when the text is so easy that the child can read sections independently. Then the child signals to the parent to remain quiet (for example, by a gentle nudge) and reads alone until a difficult word is encountered. The parent now models the word for the child and they continue to read together until the child feels ready to read alone and again signals with a nudge.

Studies have demonstrated the effectiveness of paired reading. But there are pitfalls. The procedure may distract attention from the appreciation of the content. Children with difficulties may also become extremely skilled at saying the words a split second after the parent has read them and may then not progress further. It is very important, therefore, that teachers and parents adapt the technique to suit the needs of the individual child.

HELPING CHILDREN WITH SPECIFIC DIFFICULTIES

Although it is now some years old, a project described by Young and Tyre (1983) is valuable in illustrating the effectiveness of these kinds of methods with children identified by 'specialists' as having marked specific learning difficulties in reading/spelling. The children were given intensive help, primarily by their parents, over a period of one year. At the end of the year the children had made gains in terms of Reading Age ranging from 1 year to 3 years.

The parents attended a day course and a teacher-researcher visited them at home at regular intervals. The children were taught by their parents for 30 minutes per day.

Initially, the children were given books which were some two years below their level of reading ability . Table 2.1 gives a brief outline of the teaching method that was followed. This took about 15 minutes. For the other 15 minutes the parents used the passages the children had read to play word games and to practise writing selected words. In this way reading went hand in hand with writing and spelling practice.

Table 2.1 DAILY READING - 15 MINUTES

1. **Talk about the pictures, the characters and the story so far** (*2 minutes*)

2. **Read the passage aloud with as much expression as possible, while running a finger along the line of print** (*about 3 minutes*).

3. **Read the passage aloud again with the child joining in, in 'chorus'. The child only needs to attempt to read each word** (*about 3 minutes*).

4. **Read the passage aloud again together, but this time pause occasionally for the child to provide the next word or phrase at points of the text when you feel reasonably certain that the child will be able to carry on** (*about 3 minutes*).

5. **The child reads the passage aloud. If she hesitates, supply the word or phrase** (*about 3 minutes*).

6. **Praise the child for joining in, for reading with expression, for supplying the right word, and for effort.**

(Adapted from Young and Tyre, 1983)

SUMMARY

It is important to make sure that there are times when the child can just relax and listen to someone read to them and, whenever possible, can communicate their own ideas by having a scribe to do their writing. Where there are difficulties with fluency and phonics, the constant repetition and help with word recognition can detract from the enjoyment of content. But to focus solely on the meaning aspects of literacy would deprive children of the means to be self-sufficient in reading and writing.

In this chapter we have emphasised the importance of:

- a positive and encouraging approach

- clear guidelines for parents, pupils and helpers

- regular opportunities for discussion and feedback

- the need to adapt particular techniques to suit the strategies of the individual

- praise and recognition for teachers and parents too!

GUIDELINES FOR PARENTS

1. Make sure the atmosphere is happy and relaxed.
2. Find a quiet place where there are no distractions.
3. Sit down together so that both can see the book.
4. Let the child hold the book or show you what to do.
5. Talk about the book and any illustrations first.
6. Talk about what has happened and what might happen next.
7. Smooth out any difficulties by reading any words your child doesn't know.
8. Talk about what you have read.
9. Give lots of praise for effort.
10. Ask for help from your teacher whenever you feel unsure.

Curl up with a book

Part II
Reading

Chapter 3

INTERACTIVE ASSESSMENT AND TEACHING

The purpose of this chapter is to help you decide which parts of the manual are relevant for a particular child. This requires you to make some checks and assessments as described below. But these checks need only be approximate as you will be able to fine-tune your impressions by observing how the child responds to your initial teaching plans. You then adjust your teaching accordingly. This is what we mean by the phrase 'interactive assessment and teaching'.

WHERE TO START

We shall begin this chapter by describing Table 3.1, a framework for making initial observations and assessments. These observations link with the teaching suggestions provided in subsequent chapters. Our aim is to help you plan an overall approach and to decide on priorities in relation to the time and resources available to you.

The starting point is a recognition that you already hold much information about the child or the children involved. In many cases you simply need to think about that information in relation to the framework provided in Table 3.1 and the assessment checks described. The assessment is based on the following activities:

- Examine the child's records, including national curriculum assessments and records of achievement.

- Read with the child and/or listen to the child read.

- Look at the child's writing or attempts at writing.

- Discuss with the child the content, likes and dislikes, strategies and approaches to both reading and writing.

- Make a few checks of the child's ability to use phonics as described in this chapter.

During the in-service courses that we have run for teachers, each participant has in turn brought along a description of a child, a tape recording of the child reading with them (and a copy of the text) and a sample of the child's writing. This has enabled us to discuss the results of the checks and assessments described below and to make initial plans of action drawing on the suggestions in this manual. The task has not required any remarkable skills or expertise but frequent reminders to:

- Trust your own intuition and judgment.

- Adjust your plans in the light of the child's response to your teaching.

- Remember that the 'feel good' factor is the most important ingredient of success.

TWO MODES OF ASSESSMENT

When children have difficulty with the mechanics of reading and writing, it is important to observe the child in two conditions. These are:

- The child's approaches when plenty of immediate assistance is available, i.e. when the child is not left to work out unknown words and when you read and write for the child. This gives you a good idea of how the child makes sense of content and how he or she communicates own meanings and ideas.

- The child's attainments when required to read and write more independently, i.e. when you observe the child's strategies with unknown words or analyse errors (mis-cues). This enables you to assess how the child copes with the print aspects of literacy.

INTRODUCING TABLE 3.1

Table 3.1 is arranged in three columns, headed **Meaning, Phonics** and **Fluency.** These are the three aspects of reading and writing around which competencies and skills are clustered as has been illustrated in Figure 1.1 of Chapter 1. Vertically the table is divided into four stages. These are positions from which it is convenient to take stock of how far the child has progressed. We recognise that teachers, Infant teachers in particular, may wish to make further subdivisions to the earlier stages. **The stages reflect levels 1 to 3 of initial reading skills in National Curriculum English.** At the time of writing, however, we are not sure in what form National Curriculum levels will be retained. We have preferred the term 'stages' rather than 'levels' as our main purpose is to cross-reference assessments to teaching suggestions in the manual. Furthermore, 'stage 1' is much easier to achieve than the curriculum 'level 1'.

The attainments required under the three headings may advance unevenly. Children may, for example, reach Stage 3 under the Meaning heading while still remaining at Stage 1 or Stage 2 under the other two headings. Conversely, some children may have developed relatively good word recognition skills although they have lost their interest in the content.

HOW TO USE TABLE 3.1

In order to decide where to begin teaching, you can **estimate** the child's stage of attainment in each of the three areas of Meaning, Phonics and Fluency. Base your estimates on the records that you have of the child and your impressions of her reading and writing. You may now feel ready to cross-reference your observations to the appropriate teaching chapters in this manual as shown in Table 3.2 on page 48. The case examples at the end of this chapter have been designed to help you.

With more time, you can check your estimates by following the assessment sequences described in this chapter. If you feel uncertain or the child does not succeed at your estimated stage, move up to an easier stage in that area. For example, if you are not sure that the child has achieved the checks at Stage 2 Phonics then try her on the Stage 1 checks. Similarly, move down to harder stages if you feel that you have underestimated the child's achievements. Note that:

- Table 3.1 gives only examples of what can be expected at the different stages, not exhaustive details of all the steps between stages.

- At Stage 1, early skills such as phonological awareness are assessed through a sequence of simple 'checks' described in this chapter.

- At Stage 2 and later, assessments are increasingly based on the child's reading and writing of continuous text.

LEARNING TO READ
Table 3.1

Symbols ✛▲❖ cross-reference to the Meaning, Phonics, Fluency checks in the text.

	MEANING	PHONICS	FLUENCY
STAGE 1 Early development	✛ Enjoys and joins in reading and discussion of stories ✛ Understands vocabulary of reading and writing	▲ Recognises rhymes and rhyming words ▲ Blends sounds into words ▲ Can play 'I Spy'	❖ Matches words by sight ❖ Matches letters by sight ❖ Identifies some words by sight
STAGE 2 Beginning to read and write independently	✛ Expects own reading to make sense ✛ Uses context and initial letters in working out meaning	Can read and write: ▲ single letter sounds; ▲ words such as it, at, hat, sun, dog, lid, net, cup, red, bus	❖ Reads some 100 words fluently from initial books
STAGE 3 Becoming competent	✛ Uses context to understand and predict meaning and to help with more complex phonics	▲ Can read and write words with: • consonant blends • consonant digraphs • vowel digraphs • silent 'e' *See note 4 below*	❖ Extensive and increasing sight vocabulary from books read
STAGE 4 Basic competencies achieved	✛ Context and phonological cues are used automatically in combination ✛ Selects books suitable to interests and needs	▲ Reads and writes words with more advanced phonics: • silent letters • longer word endings • polysyllabic words *See note 4 below*	❖ Reads and writes all commonly used words with ease

Notes:
1 *An initial assessment based on the framework of 'stages' of reading enables teachers to locate relevant teaching suggestions in the manual.*
2 *The items in each stage describe the end point of that stage.*
3 *The stages of reading incorporate levels 1 to 3 of initial reading skills in National Curriculum English.*
4 *Lists of words which illustrate phonics terminology are provided on pages 125 to 129*

CASE EXAMPLES

To help you to become familiar with the Stages, we have assembled five brief case examples at the end of this chapter (page 49). We suggest that you photocopy Table 3.1, so that you can refer to it when reading through the cases.

You may see similarities between these children and some of the children you teach. You may find that your observations of a particular child resemble one of the case examples. You can then adapt the initial plans of action outlined in that case example to fit the child that you are teaching.

CHECKS AND ASSESSMENTS FOR THE FOUR STAGES

STAGE 1: EARLY DEVELOPMENT

MEANING

✛ Enjoys and joins in reading and discussion of stories (Stage 1)

Does the child

- talk about stories being read to her?
- refer to the illustrations?
- guess what might happen next in the story?
- retell the story from the pictures or with prompts?
- pick up books and 'play read'?

Standard of performance
A positive response to the attraction of books is essential before skills of fluency and phonics can have any application. Learning letter-sounds and sight words are still useful activities at this stage, as long as they are treated separately as games in their own right. Their usefulness in accurate reading will become apparent to the child later.

Focus for teaching
Sharing of books, with the emphasis on pleasure and relaxation, is the first priority here, whether the child is a new beginner, or an older child who feels 'turned off' books. See Chapters 2 and 4.

+ Understands vocabulary of reading and writing (Stage 1)

Instructions: While reading a book with the child, check that she understands 'book terminology' as listed in the table below.

Standard of performance
This is not critical. As long as the child starts at the beginning, and scans line by line from left to right, only the first five items in the list are essential in the earliest stages.

Focus for teaching
More incidental references to this vocabulary are needed during shared reading time if the child's knowledge of the terms is to improve. See Chapter 2 page 18.

VOCABULARY OF READING

- What's the name of this story?
- Can you show me where it says that?
- Where does the story begin?
- Show me the front of the book
- Show me a word
- Show me the back of the book
- Show me the first page
- Show me the last page
- Point to the top of the page
- Point to the bottom of the page
- Can the child point under each word as you read?

PHONICS

At Stage One, we are concerned with phonemic awareness only and no print is involved in the assessment.

▲ Recognizes rhymes and rhyming words (Stage 1)

The ability to distinguish between rhyming and non-rhyming pairs of words is considered an important precursor to the development of further phonic skills. The checks below will enable you to decide whether the child needs to undertake the more detailed assessment and teaching described in Chapter 6.

Materials: Select a set of 12 pictures representing objects in rhyming pairs from page 100 at the end of Chapter 6. For example: pan, man; sock, lock; moon, spoon...

Instructions: In order to explain the concept of rhyming use couplets from nursery rhymes, for example:

"Humpty Dumpty sat on a wall, Humpty Dumpty had a great ...." (Sing or say some more together.)

Then say: "Jack and Jill went up the road." Let the child correct you. Take turns to say words which rhyme with 'hill', e.g. pill, will, sill, till, mill...

Now start the checks with the pictures:

Spread the 12 cards on the table randomly.

"Let's look at these picture cards. What are they?"

Agree on the names of the objects.

"Help me find the words that go together."

Demonstrate by picking out the first pair yourself.

Standard of Performance:

All five remaining pairs matched accurately.

Focus for Teaching:

Page 85 in Chapter 6 provides suggestions for teaching rhyme awareness.

▲ Blends sounds into words (Stage 1)

Instructions:

Start with syllables and progress to strings of sounds. Say each word in distinct parts, pausing for less than a second between them, but beware of giving normally unstressed syllables their full vowel value. For example, hospital is normally pronounced like hos-pittle, not as hos-pit-al.

"Listen. I am going to say some words in bits.

See if you can guess which word I am saying."

A good starting point is the child's own name, if it is more than one syllable, for example, Ste-pha-nie , Darr-en.

Standard of performance:

9 out of 10 correctly blended.

Focus for teaching:

Teaching suggestions appear on Page 88 (Chapter 6).

```
SAMPLE WORDS FOR BLENDING

1 gar-den            6 m-ou-se

2 yel-low            7 tr-ai-n

3 te-le-phone        8 sch-oo-l

4 kan-ga-roo         9 cr-a-sh

5 spr-ing           10 s-u-n
```

▲ Can play 'I Spy' (Stage 1)

The purpose of the 'I Spy' game is to determine whether the child can isolate initial letter sounds in spoken words. Researchers have called this alliteration or awareness of 'onset'.

Materials: Set of seven pictures of objects each beginning with a different sound, for example, *car, doll, fork, pencil, book, soap, mirror*. Pictures are provided on page 103 at the end of Chapter 6. Place the pictures on the table randomly.
Instructions: Agree on the names of the objects represented by the pictures. Then, "I spy ... something beginning with d". Always use the letter sound not the alphabetical name of the letter. Follow this procedure for each of the objects, repeating some more than once, so that the child is not able to give the right answer by narrowing the choice to those objects which have not been mentioned. Now reverse roles so that the child instructs the teacher with 'I Spy ..' and shows that he or she can give the initial sound for the objects on the table.

Standard of performance:
The child can identify all seven initial letter sounds both as respondent and as 'teacher'.

Focus for teaching: See page 89 in Chapter 6 for detailed teaching suggestions.

FLUENCY

❖ Matches words by sight (Stage 1)

Materials:
About five familiar words written on two separate cards (e.g. playing, house, mum, big, is). Up to ten words may be used with an older child. You may wish to prepare a second set of five cards to provide a further check.
Instructions: Ask the child to pair up the cards. "Can you find a word that looks exactly the same as this one?"

Standard of performance:
All words correctly matched.

Focus for teaching:
The child who cannot match words with distinct shapes is probably very immature, and not yet ready to learn formally. Further investigation is required which takes account of overall language development, vision and the child's performance on easy jigsaw puzzles.

❖ Matches letters by sight (Stage 1)

Materials:
Present five letters each printed on two separate cards
(for example, a, d, g, s, i).

Instructions:
"Can you find a letter that looks exactly the same as this one?"
Ask the child to pair up the cards. Add further letters, including those with similar shapes (a/o/c; l/i; b/d/p; f/t; m/w; n/u).
Note which, if any, are wrongly classified as identical.
Do not at this stage expect the child to be able to name the letters.

Standard of performance:
Five out of five on distinct shapes in the first set. Any dissimilar letters which the child classifies as the same need to be noted.
Focus for teaching: If the child is unable to match the first easy set then there is need for further investigation as outlined in the word matching task. Discrimination of letters with similar shapes will be learnt through handwriting (page 162 in Chapter 9) and through the illustrated letter cards (Chapter 6, page 108).

❖   Identifies some words by sight (Stage 1)

Can the child read at sight words which have been read repeatedly with her?
Materials: Present four or five cards with familiar words written on them, for example, the child's own name and the names of characters from a familiar book. Display pictures of the characters if possible.
Instructions: Point to the words as you read them for the child. Now mix up the cards and ask the child to read them for you.

Standard of performance:
All correct.

Focus for teaching:
See the case example of William on page 71 in Chapter 5.

N.B. The standards of performance for the checks at Stage 1 are based on our own judgments and experience. They can be altered according to the   teacher's judgment. Please remember that the items for each stage in Table 3.1 represent the end point of that stage indicating that the child is ready to move on to the next stage.

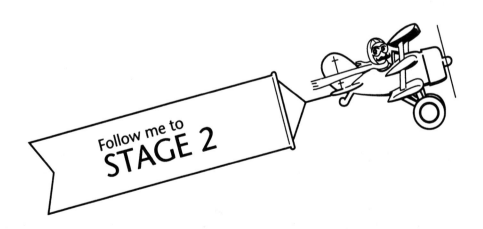

STAGE 2: BEGINNING TO READ AND WRITE INDEPENDENTLY

Most of the assessment at Stage 2 and beyond is done informally, as part of the regular teaching and monitoring process, while reading and writing with the child. Where a child is experiencing difficulty, more detailed checks are often best constructed by the teacher to fit in with the vocabulary and structure of the reading. Examples of assessments given here are for guidance only, and may be used as a pattern of approach, the teacher substituting her own materials.

MEANING

✛   **Expects own reading to make sense (Stage 2)**

✛   **Uses context and initial letters
    in working out meaning (Stage 2)**

When sharing a book with you, does the child:

- look for meaning first by scanning illustrations and other cues?
- hesitate over misreadings which do not make sense?
- use pictures, context and initial letters as aids to working out the meaning of unfamiliar words?
- re-read the line or first part of the sentence to help with working out an unfamiliar word?
- comment on events or characters in the story?

    Standard of performance:

    All the above aspects of attention to meaning should be well understood and habitual.

    Focus for teaching:
    Repeated demonstration and practice while sharing books. See Chapter 4 page 57.

PHONICS

▲ Can read and write single letter sounds (Stage 2)

Does the child know the sounds of all letters of the alphabet?
Test by showing letter cards (lower-case), one at a time, or letters written in a random order on a sheet of paper and asking the child
"What sound is this?"
Now dictate the letter sounds, again in a random order.

Standard of performance:
All correct.

Record errors and confusion (e.g. b/d/p/; u/n; m/w; f/t).

Focus for teaching:
If the child knows few letter sounds, start teaching from page 91 in Chapter 6. If there are only some errors or confusions, focus on those through spelling (Chapter 9) and handwriting (Chapter 10).

Note:
The National Curriculum requires children to know the alphabet. This can be misleading if they try to sound out words using alphabet names instead of sounds. It is necessary to teach that letters have names as well as sounds. We have omitted checks of letter names at this stage but some teachers may wish to include them. Capital Letters can also be tested and taught in the same way as lower case letters.

▲ Can read and write words such as *it, at, hat, sun, dog, lid, net, cup, red, bus* (Stage 2)

Can the child blend sounds into words?

At this stage the test is confined to Vowel-Consonant [V-C] and Consonant-Vowel-Consonant [C-V-C] words. Present, one at a time, a set of up to twenty words, written individually on cards. (For example, in, at, up, on, let, man, fox, hen, jam, pig, net, sad, ran, wet, bus, cat, lid, pot, gun, hat.) Or substitute your own set of words. Examples of phonologically regular words are provided at the end of Chapter 7, page 126. If the child can read the words, select 10 of them for dictation.

Standard of performance:
At least 18 correctly read and 9 correctly spelt. Note any letters not recognised, or called by alphabet names rather than sounds.

Focus for teaching:
See page 95 in Chapter 6.

FLUENCY

❖ Reads some 100 words fluently from initial books (Stage 2)

Fluency is assessed informally as you listen to the child read. Make sure that the book is appropriate, i.e. that it is at an 'instructional' level. If you find that the child struggles with nearly every word, you need to join in with him or her and read together. Otherwise the child will become discouraged. Many teachers find that cataloguing books by readability levels is helpful and refer to the NASEN A-Z Graded List of Reading Books (see page 198) or the framework of levels described by particular reading schemes.

The suggestion that the child should recognize some 100 words immediately and fluently at sight is arbitrary but in our experience it is a reasonable number to aim for as an indication that the child has reached the end of Stage 2. There is no need to count the words exactly or to make a list of them. Also observe the child's own writing: to what extent are words that he or she can read also spelt correctly?

Standard of performance:
Immediate and automatic word recognition.

Focus for teaching:
Chapter 4 provides general teaching suggestions for developing fluency. These link well with the parallel spelling practice as described in Chapter 8 page 137. The Step-by-step approach in Chapter 5 is designed for those children who are at the very beginning of Stage 2, i.e. whose reading vocabulary is very limited.

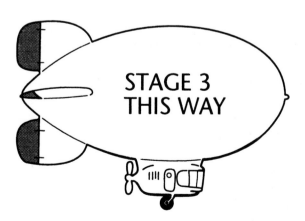

STAGE 3: BECOMING COMPETENT

MEANING and PHONICS and FLUENCY

✦ Uses context to understand and predict meaning and to help with more complex phonics (Stage 3)

By this stage it is difficult to separate out Meaning, Phonics and Fluency as distinct areas. The main characteristic of the Stage 3 reader is the way these areas are combined through:

- self-correction;
- increasing confidence in making informed guesses, based on a combination of context, recognition of whole words, and phonics;
- where there is a difficult word, reading on to the end of a sentence to see what word might make sense;
- using knowledge gained from other sources when tackling unknown words;
- checking that guesses fit in with the appearance of the word;
- seeing 'little words in big words', e.g. book-shop, black-board;
- analysing words by letter-strings or syllables rather than letter by letter;
- a greatly increased and increasing sight vocabulary;
- a more expressive reading voice.

▲ Can read and write words with: consonant blends, consonant digraphs, vowel digraphs, silent 'e' (Stage 3)

The quickest way to check is to construct a spelling test drawing on words listed at the end of Chapter 7 page 125. Three words from each group presented in a random order should be sufficient. Bear in mind, however, that children may perform quite well on a spelling test consisting of lists of words without using that knowledge in their normal reading and writing. You really need to hear the child read and observe his or her free writing in order to confirm your impressions from the screening check. A system for noting and analysing errors (mis-cues) is described below (page 45).

Standard of performance:
Note which combinations need to be taught or need further consolidation.

Focus for teaching:
see Chapter 7 for phonics and Chapter 8 for spelling.

❖ Extensive and increasing sight vocabulary from books read (Stage 3)

As with Stage 2, it is the immediate and fluent recognition of words that is being examined. Some children may develop a slow and halting reading style which relies heavily on phonics and context. In the parallel area of spelling, they may spell common words in a phonologically predictable way rather than in their visually correct form.

Standard of performance:
It is not possible to give exact criteria. It is the style and strategies for reading and writing that matter.

Focus for teaching:
Chapters 2 and 4 provide ideas for building up fluency. Chapter 8 suggests methods of learning spelling and has an initial list of the most commonly used words.

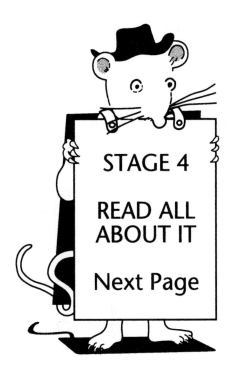

STAGE 4

READ ALL
ABOUT IT

Next Page

STAGE 4: BASIC COMPETENCIES ACHIEVED

MEANING

✚ **Context and phonological cues are used automatically in combination (Stage 4)**

Stage 4 is an extension of Stage 3 involving more complex content and vocabulary. The dividing line between these two stages is arbitrary; it is not clear when exactly the child moves from one to the next. Teaching increasingly focuses on the areas of information handling and response to literature as described in national curriculum English.

PHONICS and FLUENCY

▲ **Reads and writes words with more advanced phonics: silent letters, longer word endings, polysyllabic words (Stage 4)**

❖ **Reads and writes commonly used words fluently and with ease (Stage 4)**

The listing of particular phonological regularities under Stage 4 is a matter of opinion. Some would say that they belong to Stage 3 or even earlier. For example, compound words such as *countryside* or *knowledge*, when split into their component shorter words, may well be taught earlier. As in Stage 3, the quickest way to check the child's attainments in phonics is to construct a spelling test drawing on words listed from page 125. But you need to confirm the results through observing the child's reading strategies and free writing.

> **Standard of performance:**
> At the end of Stage 4 basic competencies are well established.

> **Focus for teaching:**
> Those children making slow progress within Stage 4 may benefit from the suggestions in the second half of Chapter 7 (phonics), Chapter 8 (spelling) and Chapter 9 (handwriting).

CLASSIFYING ERRORS (Miscues)
when hearing the child read

The fluent Stage 3 or Stage 4 reader expects the content to make sense and uses context as an aid to identify unfamiliar words. Phonics in turn are used to check contextual cues by looking at word structure in terms of elements of meaning (e.g. horse-shoe not horses-hoe); syllables (e.g. pho-to-graph) and letter-strings (e.g. str-eng-th). By noting down errors when hearing the child read, we can determine to what extent he or she is using these strategies and which aspects still need careful teaching.

For the purpose of examining errors a slightly more difficult text can be chosen. Ideally the child's reading should be tape recorded for later analysis and errors marked on a copy of the text. The following are some usual ways of marking errors.

SOME WAYS TO MARK ERRORS (MIS-CUES) WHEN HEARING THE CHILD READ.

The trees in the f~~or~~est cast long shadows on the

ground. It was very(peaceful.)The children sat

under the tree reading their books.

fo~~r~~est (substitution)

(peaceful)(circle non-response)

ch-ild-ren (phonic strategy noted)

tick for self-corrections ✓

Consider these three questions
- **Does the child expect to make sense of the text?**
- **What does the child do when confronted by an unknown word?**
- **How fluently does the child read?**

Examples taken from longer text analyses

The following examples are extracts from much longer texts. They have been chosen to illustrate the process of planning teaching from observation of errors.

Debbie:	*'What happy noo?'*
Text:	What happens now?

Teacher's notes:
Debbie does not seem to expect meaning. She substitutes with a real word which has the same initial letter (happy/happens). The second substitution also has the correct initial letter but it is a nonsense word (noo/now). *Phonics:* Debbie seems to know and use initial letter sounds. Is she confusing ow and oo?
Action: Debbie needs to talk about the story and predict the content before reading it. When reading together, Debbie's teacher or parent can scan ahead and help her guess appropriate words, e.g. 'the girl went out to pl..'. Phonics such as initial consonant blends can be introduced in the context of words which appear in her book.

Robin:	*'We have e-n-o-u-g-h enough m-o-n-e-y money to get s-w-e-e-t-s sweets'* (letter-by-letter sounding).
Text:	We haven't enough money to buy sweets.

Teacher's notes:
Robin has developed a habit of sounding each letter before he makes a guess. The sounding out is inefficient and hinders reading fluency. Yet remarkably, he reads the words correctly. Robin seems unwilling to take a risk with guessing whole words. His caution may be justified in view of the reading of 'haven't' as 'have' and 'buy' as 'get'.

Action:
Encourage contextual guessing. Repeated reading of an easier text should improve fluency. Teach phonically regular words as spellings using the look-cover-write-check procedure (see Chapter 8) and memorise difficult bits such as '-ough' as spelling patterns. It is important to make sure that Robin practises new words until they are read fluently and without hesitation.

Jane: *'He could not s... for he was hot. The children tired to,*
             too tired pull him as ...'

Text: He could not swim for he was hurt. The children tried
             to pull him ashore.

Teacher's notes:
Jane relies almost entirely on sight words and tries to make some sense of the story.
Her phonic knowledge is weak, e.g. sw in 'swim', ur in 'hurt', tr in 'tried'.
Action:
Check blends and digraphs using the phonic checklist on page 116 and follow the
methods of teaching described in Chapter 7. Reassess Jane's performance on a
more interesting text.

Uneven development

The examples above illustrate some patters of uneven development in the three
areas of meaning, phonics and fluency . As described in Chapter 1, we consider the
areas to have a 'multiplying' effect through the interaction between them. We
assume that the reader simultaneously synthesizes information from previous
experience, knowledge of meaning and grammar, and visual and phonic
information. Although one area can to some extent compensate for another,
children may develop habits of over-reliance on one of them at the expense of the
others. As you listen to the child read, look out for the following patterns:

- **Over-reliance on meaning:** the child depends too much on context and
  meaning without sufficient backup from the other two areas. The child
  may read quite fast, but the reading bears little relation to the actual words
  on the page. There is a need to focus more on the areas of phonics and
  fluency without losing sight of the strengths that the child already has in
  the area of meaning.

- **Over-reliance on phonics:** the child reads haltingly sounding out every
  word. Here we need to emphasise the other two areas, i.e. meaning and
  fluency as described in Chapter 2 and Chapter 4. Plenty of assisted reading
  of content that is of interest to the child will be one way forward.

- **Over-reliance on fluency:** the child either reads a word at once or not at all.
  The child has few strategies for tackling unknown words through a
  combination of context and phonics. Here the relevant chapters on phonics
  and meaning need to be combined. For example, when reading together, the
  teacher will scan ahead for familiar phonic combination and help the child to
  read these words in context.

SUMMARY

The purpose of this chapter has been to help you decide which parts of the manual are relevant for a particular child. There are two ways, or a combination of the two, that you might have followed in undertaking this task:

- **The quicker way:**
  You compared your previous knowledge and observations of the child with the stages outlined in Table 3.1 (page 32) and estimated the child's stages of attainment. You then photocopied Table 3.1 and read through some of the case examples at the end of this chapter in order to find how the stages linked with initial plans of action under the three headings of 'Meaning', 'Phonics' and 'Fluency'. You may have found similarities between your observations of a particular child and one of the case examples, and you may then have adapted the initial plans of action outlined in that case example to fit the child that you are teaching.

- **The thorough way:**
  Given more time, you worked through the appropriate checks and assessments for the child concerned. You formed a more detailed picture of the child's achievements and strategies, and noted down the chapter or page numbers referred to at the end of each assessment. On the basis of this work, you formulated your own initial plans of action under the three headings of 'Meaning', 'Phonics' and 'Fluency'.

For both methods of initial assessment, Table 3.2 below shows which chapters have priority at the different stages of learning. The focus on meaning in Chapter 2 is common to all stages as it provides the foundations for learning. After that, the sequence of chapters reflects growing competence and independence in basic literacy. Some chapters are relevant to more than one stage, illustating the overlap between them.

Spelling and handwriting have their own sequences of development which parallel those of reading. Although spelling closely mirrors reading and is indeed identical at Stage 1, the particular teaching suggestions in these chapters need to be combined with the suggestions made in the chapters concerned with reading.

TABLE 3.2 PRIORITY CHAPTERS

All stages	1.	An overview of the manual
	2.	A focus on meaning
Stage 1	5.	Step-by-step teaching
	6.	Phonics at Stages 1 and 2
Stage 2	4.	Developing fluency
	5.	Step-by-step teaching
	6.	Phonics at Stages 1 and 2
	8.	Spelling
	9.	Handwriting
Stage 3	4.	Developing fluency
	7.	Phonics at Stages 3 and 4
	8.	Spelling
	9.	Handwriting
Stage 4	7.	Phonics at Stages 3 and 4
	8.	Spelling
	9.	Handwriting

EXAMPLES OF INITIAL PLANS OF ACTION

This section links directly with Table 3.1. A selection of brief examples, drawn from longer case studies, illustrate the initial assessment and planning that has been described in some detail in this chapter. We suggest that you photocopy Table 3.1 (page 32), so that you can refer to it while reading through the cases. The cases have in common:

- assessment and planning under the three headings of Meaning, Phonics and Fluency;

- the setting of priorities in the light of the child's particular strengths and needs and the time/resources available;

- cross-referencing to relevant sections in this manual to draw up an initial plan.

You may see similarities between these children and some of the children you teach. You may find that your observations of a particular child resemble one of the case examples below. You can then adapt the initial plans of action outlined in that case examples to fit the child that you are teaching.

Please note that in the **plans of action**, many of the activities are suitable for use with small groups of children, and may not require the constant involvement of the teacher.

TINA (aged 6.6 years; Year 2)

Having followed the checks and assessments based on Table 3.1 Tina's teacher has formed the following initial impressions:

MEANING

Stage 1 achieved: Tina joins in reading and discussion of stories. She understands the vocabulary of reading and writing. **Stage 2** not learnt.

PHONICS

Stage 1 Tina does not pass the 'I Spy' check but shows that she has the phonic skills required by the other two checks. **Stage 2** not started

FLUENCY

Stage 1 skills learnt: Tina matches words and letters. **Stage 2** not learnt: Tina can recognise very few words reliably, immediately and fluently.

INITIAL PLAN OF ACTION

Meaning Stage 2: Continue with assisted reading of as many books as possible which have been chosen by Tina.
(see page 23 in Chapter 2 and page 57 in Chapter 4).

Phonics Stage 1: Systematic practice, involving both reading and writing, of initial letter sounds through activities such as the modified 'I spy' game and the illustrated alphabet (see pages 91 and 108 in Chapter 6).

Fluency Stage 2: A programme of repetitive reading and writing of a limited number of 'sight' words until they have really been mastered (see page 72 in Chapter 5).

PRIORITIES

For her 'five-minutes-per-day' plan Tina's teacher decides to focus at this stage on the Phonics tasks. She is fortunate in having the assistance of a voluntary classroom helper and the support of Tina's father in following the suggestions under the Meaning heading. Because of the limited time available to her, the Fluency tasks are at present held 'on ice' but will be reconsidered later in the light of the progress Tina is making. (N.B. These were the choices made by Tina's teacher. Other alternatives could have been equally valid such as a focus on Fluency as described in the case study of William on page 71. It is Tina's response to the teaching which determines whether these choices were appropriate for her .)

RASHID (aged 6 years; Year 2)

Rashid has learnt English at school. His teacher speaks only English but finds that she can now hold quite a fluent conversation with him. Rashid can recognise several words in reading but is not progressing as well as the other children in the class. His teacher makes observations as she reads and writes with him, and does some of the Phonics checks for Stage 1.

MEANING

Stage 1: Rashid much prefers activities other than reading and writing.
He is unsure of the vocabulary of reading.

Stage 2: Rashid does not seem to expect his reading to make sense.

PHONICS

Stage 1: Rhymes and 'I Spy ' are uncertain.

Stage 2: Rashid's own writing shows some appropriate use of single letters but he does not have enough knowledge to be able to undertake the checks for this stage.

FLUENCY

Stage 1 achieved: Rashid also recognises his own name, friends' names, labels in class.

Stage 2: Rashid recognises by sight some 20 words.

INITIAL PLAN OF ACTION

Meaning Stage 1:
(a) Find out whether Rashid is having literacy lessons in his mother tongue and what progress he is making. Rashid's mother, who is also learning English, may wish to share the same books with him, and talk to him about the pictures and story in both English and their first language (see page 27 in Chapter 2).
(b) Arrange opportunities for Rashid to dictate stories and use these as a reading book (see page 59 in Chapter 4). While reading and writing with Rashid, emphasise the concepts and vocabulary involved (see page 18 in Chapter 2).
(c) Find books that Rashid will positively enjoy. Enlist support from voluntary helpers in class to share books with Rashid, emphasising fun and involvement.

Phonics Stage 1: Involve Rashid with other children in playing rhyming games and I Spy . Depending on his response to these group activities, start planning a more systematic approach based on Chapter 6.

Fluency Stage 2: Continue to develop sight vocabulary through shared story writing and the kinds of activities described in Chapter 4.

DAVID (aged 8 years; Year 3)

David is a quiet child, anxious to get things right, and shy about asking for help. His teacher realises that he has been slipping through the net, and begins over a period to make careful observations about his reading and writing. When she finds that he has difficulty with some of the Stage 2 Phonics assessments, she checks him on Stage 1 Oral Sound Blending, and finds he has not progressed from there.

MEANING

Stage 2: Enjoys reading with the teacher, but lacks confidence when reading alone.

Relies largely on pictures and sight words – sometimes gives a paraphrase of the story.

PHONICS

Stage 1: Blends sounds into words only when spoken by teacher.

Stage 2: Can read and write most single sounds (not w, y: Confuses b/d; n/u; m/w; f/t.) Can sound out words, but not blend them. Spelling: Asks for most words.

FLUENCY

Stage 2: Knows about 40 words. This knowledge is slow to increase.

Handwriting: Very slow. 'Draws' letters incorrectly and laboriously. Confuses b/d.

INITIAL PLAN OF ACTION

Meaning Stage 2: Adopt a three-pronged plan:
(a) David's parents are very willing to continue sharing with him books of David's choice, paying particular attention to the story as described in Chapter 2 (page 27).
(b) Let David listen to short stories on tape, following the text in the book until he has really mastered the text at an independent level (see Chapter 4 page 62).
(c) Encourage David to re-read to friends some of the books he already knows, to reinforce vocabulary and remind him of his success .
Fluency Stage 2: Select a book for intensive repetition and learning of sight vocabulary (see Chapter 5).
Phonics Stage 2: Demonstrate 'how words work' by showing David how to analyse simple words in his sight vocabulary, as described in Chapter 6 Phonics on page 98.
Teach letters confused in conjunction with handwriting (see Chapter 9 page 160 for details).
Composition: Organise group writing activities so that David works with two other children, and can contribute ideas without being under pressure at this stage to do the scribing.

Handwriting: Encourage a relaxed, fluent approach with large-scale writing patterns in paint and thick crayon. When introducing cursive writing, emphasise flow and reasonable speed. Teach b/d etc by associating letter-sound and handwritten shape, following the procedure in Chapter 9 (Handwriting).

Spelling: Teach spelling of words along with phonics (as above) at this stage as described in Chapter 6 page 95.

PRIORITIES

This action plan cannot be adopted immediately in its entirety. His teacher's priorities are: to build up David's confidence through shared activities; to teach systematically a small sight vocabulary; to teach how blending works.

MATTHEW (aged 9 years; Year 4)

Matthew reads and enjoys books such as The Hobbit. His written work is, in contrast, less well developed. The teacher looks at his writing in the context of Table 3.1.

MEANING

Stage 4 : Largely achieved in reading although Matthew's reading style is somewhat inaccurate involving frequent self-correction.

Composition: Writes quickly without planning. Little variation in sentences.

PHONICS

Stage 4: Works out more advanced phonics when reading unfamiliar words.

Spelling: Inconsistent, sometimes unintelligible. Vowels often misrepresented.

FLUENCY

Stage 4: Reads most words fluently.

Handwriting: Correctly formed, unjoined, uneven, fast. Omits spaces between words.

INITIAL PLAN OF ACTION

Meaning: Work with Matthew in a group with other children on planning and drafting.

Fluency: (Handwriting): Planning his work should help to assure Matthew that he will not forget his ideas before he gets them down, and that he can therefore take more time over presentation. Re-introduce joined writing as described in Chapter 9. Other children in the class may also benefit from this instruction.

Spelling: Show Matthew how to read through his work when he has finished to check for obvious spelling errors (Chapter 8, page 142).
Introduce the 'vowel-sound dictionary' (Chapter 8 page 149) to help Matthew to listen to, analyse, and reproduce short vowel sounds.
Start a concentrated spelling programme based on his errors (Chapter 8, page 145).
Check whether he can use a dictionary efficiently, and make sure it is on his table when he is writing.

EMMA (aged 10 years; Year 6)

Emma has been receiving extra help with reading and spelling for two years, and has made good progress. Her teacher reviews Emma's class work over a period, and refers to Table 3.1 when making her summary and Action Plans.

MEANING

Stage 4 well on the way. Uses context and phonic cues consciously, not automatically. Persistent: re-reads a sentence until satisfied with the meaning.

Composition. Writes long , well constructed stories and accounts.

PHONICS

Stage 3 : Knows and applies many rules, but not confident. Looks to contextual support for confirmation.

Spelling: Checks work, uses Spelling Dictionary, but still has great problems with even common words.

FLUENCY

Stage 3: Often needs to give herself Phonic prompts. Confuses common words when reading difficult texts (what/that; and/said).

Handwriting. Quick and well presented.

CONTINUING PLAN OF ACTION

Meaning: Teach Emma to scan a book before selecting it, and skim the text before reading for clues to the structure and meaning, looking at pictures, diagrams, captions, subheadings, highlighted words.

Fluency: Show her (and other competent readers) how to help less advanced children with their reading. This will have the additional advantage of giving Emma more practice in fluent reading of easier texts.

Phonics: Helping other children should reinforce Emma's phonic skills. Teach new combinations through Spelling.

Spelling: Introduce the Spell-check on the computer.
Continue Spelling study programme:

- Teach by using augmented Look-Cover-Write-Check procedure.
- Confirm that she edits her work after writing.
- Use her own writing as a source of new words to learn.
- Base word-family groups on these spellings where possible.
- Constantly revise previous spelling work through sentence making and dictation

(All these aspects are covered in Chapter 8)

Chapter 4

DEVELOPING FLUENCY

Initial difficulties easily lead to avoidance of reading and writing which, in turn, prevents progress. This chapter considers ways of increasing opportunities for rehearsal and repetition of familiar texts in order to consolidate learning while retaining the learner's interest and sense of success.

INTRODUCTION

In this chapter we describe how children can learn to recognise the vocabulary of a book by reading it repeatedly, and by using a variety of supplementary materials to practise the words so that they are retained. We recommend that repeated reading and supplementary activities be carried out in parallel with assisted reading of a wider range of books, where the teacher or parent shares books with the child as described in Chapter 2.

Provided that much of the reading vocabulary of a book is familiar to the learner, the advantage of a repetitive approach is that skills already mastered receive further practice, while new learning takes place through increased rehearsal and repetition of the content. In addition, the child has the opportunity to acquire other reading and writing skills incidentally.

The child who has great difficulty in remembering words needs to be given specific learning tasks, and provision for practising these tasks until they are mastered. This way of planning and teaching is outlined in the next chapter (Chapter 5). In the present chapter we describe more general ways of increasing rehearsal and repetition through tasks which involve:

- Prepared reading

- Repetition through written activities

- The use of tape recorders and microcomputers

PREPARED READING

Children who have experienced difficulties in learning to read and write are likely to associate books with failure and frustration. The teacher's first task is to help them to find pleasure and success in books. This is best achieved by letting the child select a 'new' book at the appropriate stage (see Chapter 3) and using the book in such a way that the pupil cannot fail to read it well. The following activities, based on suggestions provided by Muriel Bridge, are designed to ensure successful reading. Note that all activites relate to the vocabulary of the selected book.

Preparation before reading

Before the child makes an attempt to read the book, the teacher discusses it in such a way as to arouse interest, and forestall the most predictable difficulties. She starts by commenting on the title of the book, and encouraging the child to examine the pictures and text for clues to the meaning. The aim is to foster a positive attitude towards the book, and to help the child to predict the content, sentences, and individual words. The teacher might say:

> *"Let's look at the new book we have chosen.*
> *It's called 'Margaret's Secret'. Can you see that written here on the*
> *cover?*
> *Look at the first picture. Which one do you think is Margaret?*
> *What's that on the table in the picture?*
> *Look at the writing on this page and try to find the name Margaret.*
> *Good! and here it is again.*
> *This says Mrs Blenkinsop. I wonder who she is?*
> *And here's the word for that thing on the table. What did you say it*
> *was? That's right. It's a pineapple.*
> *Now let's look at the pictures and see if we can guess what happens in*
> *the story."*

The first reading

If the child is expected to master the vocabulary by spending a considerable time on the book, it should be interesting enough to merit close attention. The teacher may well choose to read it to the whole class, thus establishing the book as a worthwhile story, and alleviating any sense of shame the child may have about being on an 'easy' book.

When reading with the individual child, the teacher pauses before predictable words or phrases to give him an opportunity to guess from context, or work out from phonics what comes next. Sometimes a whole word, or all but the first letter or digraph is covered, encouraging the child to pay attention to meaning, and guess. If an appropriate answer is not supplied within a few seconds, the teacher reads on smoothly. The experience is unhurried and enjoyable, with attention to meaning rather than learning or testing.

Alternatively the teacher may make a tape recording of a frequently used book, pausing before occasional words to allow the pupil to guess what comes next. The child follows the text, and supplies the missing word from context or phonics. Suggestions on how to record books on tape for children to listen to are provided in a later section of this chapter.

Subsequent readings

Paying regard to the difficulties a particular book presents to the child, teacher and pupil gradually reverse roles on subsequent readings. The second time, the pupil may repeat a page that the teacher has just read, or read alternate pages with her. Where the child takes too long to work out a word, and appears in danger of losing the flow of the story, the teacher quietly prompts. To restore continuity, she may then read the next sentence or two for the child. Errors which retain the meaning need not always be corrected.

Further reading

If children experience enjoyment and success in reading the book, we hope they are willing to read it again. They may choose to read it silently to themselves or to take it home to read to parents, grandparents, and brothers and sisters. Children who do not show a spontaneous interest in re-reading the book yet again can often be persuaded to demonstrate their prowess by reading it to a younger child in school, or to parent-helpers, or students. The best kind of response the child can receive to his reading is 'Thank you for letting me hear that story. I did enjoy it'.

Play reading

Some books lend themselves to adaptation as play reading. Interest is further heightened by a specific purpose for this activity, for example, to make a tape or to perform to a group or the class. Children enjoy devising appropriate sound effects. They willingly undertake the amount of rehearsal necessary to perfect their part.

REPETITION THROUGH WRITTEN ACTIVITIES

Written and oral activities based on the book that has been read as described above have a double benefit. First, they reinforce literacy skills by focusing activities on the limited, familiar area of the chosen book. In this way the pupils' needs for a more repetitive approach are met in the context of a story which they enjoy reading, writing and talking about. Second, teacher time is released by providing semi-independent work for children.

Word strips

Word strips are useful with the child who is at the beginning of Stage 2. They are easier and more meaningful than the traditional individual word flash cards. Flash cards present the child with the kind of memory task which does not allow them to take advantage of linguistic cues, and we would not usually recommend them.

To create a word strip, a phrase or short sentence is taken from the book. Children might like to choose the sentence. They copy this boldly onto a small strip of card. Allow about 4cm per word, with the card 3cm deep. Initially the child may need help with the copying, for example, the teacher may mark off word spaces or write the words in faintly so that the child can trace over them. The teacher then proceeds as follow:

> "Do you remember what this sentence says? Read it to me again.
> Write the sentence clearly in pencil over my writing.
> Now read it again, without looking at the pictures in the book.
> Let's make it brighter. Write over the words in felt-tip (or crayon).
> Read it to me again.
> Now we are going to cut the sentence into words, and jumble them up.
> Do you think you can do that? Look at the book if you need to.
> Read the words again now, and let's see if you have made the sentence properly.
> Well done!"

A second sentence from the book may be treated in the same way. The task of re-sorting the words of two sentences is more demanding. If mistakes are made, the child re-reads the phrase or the sentence while attending more carefully to whether it makes sense. The two cut up sentences can be stored in an envelope. Pairs of subsequent sentences need to be kept in separate envelopes and identified clearly, for example by using different coloured card or felt-tip pen. If several sentences inadvertently get jumbled up, even teachers will struggle with the task of sorting them out!

Writing and drawing activities

Reading, writing and drawing can be enjoyable and mutually reinforcing. As the activities are undertaken fairly independently, however, there is a danger that the tasks may encourage mindless copying which does not develop either reading or writing skills. It is important, therefore, that the pupil always has opportunity to read the completed task with the teacher, parent or other competent reader. This should happen on repeated occasions, for example, by going over previous work before adding to it or before starting on a new task.

The following selection provides some examples of supplementary writing activities:

- The child copies out the word strip as a caption for a picture, either in an exercise book or loose-leaf folder, or as a large wall picture.

- The child chooses a favourite part from the book to illustrate and add a caption or speech ballooons derived from the text.

- The child reads and illustrates captions or speech ballooons provided by the teacher. All the words come from the reading book.

- The same treatment can be given to a series of incidents from the story or, indeed, the whole story. This requires quite sophisticated skills of remembering the entire story and selecting the main incidents in sequence. (This is suitable as a class activity and is appropriate to any level. The children can produce a group zig-zag book, or individual comic strip versions.)

- Pupils might like to imagine that they are a character in the book and rewrite part or all of the story in the first person. The children then use the published book as a 'dictionary' to look up words and phrases whenever necessary. They may have to rehearse the account orally, helped by their teacher, before they are able to write it.

- The pupil imagines what happens either before or after the story in the book and speaks/writes/draws the ideas.

- Some stories lend themselves to map making. Pupils label or make up a key for the incidents on their maps.

Additional workbooks or worksheets

Many publishers of reading materials provide additional workbooks to reinforce the vocabulary that has been covered in a particular book. Although they are sometimes a useful resource, workbooks do not necessarily fit the learning needs of the individual child. They do not always provide sufficient repetition. Most important, these workbooks do not on their own enhance reading and writing skills as children will benefit only if there is sufficient opportunity to read the text with the teacher, the parent or another child. Without that active learning, many of the tasks in the workbooks may demand nothing more than visual matching and copying, and amount to a time-filling occupation.

Making up your own additional worksheets together with the child can be much more rewarding. Don't worry about your drawing skills . We are not asking you or the child to produce works of art but to concentrate on the written communication involved. Children may wish to design worksheets for each other, thus providing themselves with further opportunities to look up and write the vocabulary covered in the book. The additional practice might include a selection from the following kinds of activities:

- **FILLING IN THE MISSING WORD:** The teacher or the child makes up sentences based on the content of the chosen book. Occasional words are missed out and a space or a line is drawn instead. The task of filling in the missing word can be made easier if an initial letter cue is provided or if there is a choice of, say, three words and only one of them fits the meaning of the sentence, for example:

  > *ran*
  > *Johnny rope to the pond to help.*
  > *red*

- **YES/NO QUESTIONS,** e.g. *'Did the sun shine in the park?'* In completing this task the child has an opportunity to enjoy the sense of success in reading and answering questions relating to familiar content and vocabulary. There is no requirement to copy out questions or respond in writing with anything other than 'yes' or 'no'. Some children will be able to follow the teacher's example and design questions for others to complete. An ability to differentiate between the grammatical forms of statements and questions is the kind of skill required by the national curriculum.

- **SILLY SENTENCES** are a particular favourite. The teacher or the child makes up a list of sentences about the story some of which are 'silly', e.g. *'The sun is in the sea'.* The worksheet is then completed by identifying the silly sentences. The construction of sentences is also required by the English national curriculum.

- **QUESTIONS** which begin with Who did   ?', 'Who said...?', 'How did ...?', Why did ...?' Some of these questions require lengthier and more thoughtful answers than the previous types.

- **SENTENCE COMPLETION** with wording slightly different from that in the book is easier if page references are given. Make sure, however, that the child completes it through reading the sentences rather than some other strategy such as figuring out from their visual appearance which words have not been used.

- **MAKING INFERENCES:** Questions which involve the child in making inferences such as 'You can tell that ... because ...'; I liked ...(the character) because ...'; What would you do if ... (you were in the same situation as the character)?'. These questions are harder than the previous ones in that children have to project themselves into the imaginary situation.

- **LENGTHIER ASSIGNMENTS,** for example asking the child to write a letter to one of the characters or to the author of the book. The story book could lead to a widening study of picture and reference books on any related topic or setting.

TAPE RECORDERS AND MICROCOMPUTERS

Many of the supplementary activities described in the earlier parts of this chapter can be made more interesting if they are undertaken with the help of tape recorders or microcomputers. This adds a new and stimulating dimension to practising the same reading vocabulary.

Most children and teachers find the prospect of using computers and computer programs exciting, and work enthusiastically with new material. There is no guarantee, however, that the content and methods of teaching are appropriate for the learning needs of the individual. Disillusionment may set in once the novelty has worn off.

It is important to be clear about the purpose and demands of each task. It might be discussion with other pupils of an adventure story with alternative developments to choose from. Here the focus would be on the meaning and structure of the story. If, however, the intention is to provide additional reading-practice of a specific words, then targets related to these words need to be established. Because we have no other evidence of learning, it is more important when we use technical aids to keep accurate records of learning targets and achievements than it is when we are able to give the children individual teacher attention. Many programs now contain built-in ways of providing feedback and keeping records, encouraging children to compete against their own best 'scores'. The next chapter will describe principles of detailed programme planning and record keeping.

Below we provide some suggestions for offering a repetitive approach to learning with the help of a tape recorder, and discuss briefly the use, to date, of computer programs for the teaching of reading and writing.

The tape recorder

When children listen to taped stories they cannot see the reader's facial expressions or gestures, and are deprived of this additional clue to meaning. Various techniques can be used by the teacher to compensate for the loss, for example:

- Lowering the voice, and speaking close to the microphone , across it rather into it, gives a more intimate and chatty tone.

- Speaking slowly, but retaining the phrasing of the text, especially if the child is to be required to read with the taped story.

- Emphasising rhythm by reading function words more quickly, and stressing the words with key meanings. For example: 'There is a HOUSE - - at the END - - of the ROAD.'

Reading the text in this manner, with longer pauses and heavy stresses on certain words, slows down the pace while retaining the meaning and sounding relatively natural. It is helpful to mark the text in advance by underlining words to be stressed and marking the pauses.

Reading the whole story while listening to the tape recorder requires fairly advanced skills (end of Stage 2 or Stage 3). For the beginner more detailed planning is needed, as follows:

1. Read a passage of the text slowly, with exaggerated phrasing. The child follows the text with her finger.

2. Say: 'I am going to read that again, and this time you can join in with me. Start when I say "ready". . . . Ready'. The rhythm of reading needs to be consistent so that the child knows exactly when to start and what pace to adopt.

3. Say: 'Now a little faster. Ready', and repeat the reading.

4. Say: 'I am going to read it just once more, then it's your turn. . . .Now you read'.

5. When the child feels confident of getting it right, she is ready to show off her achievement to her teacher, parent, or friend.

The above procedure would not usually be completed at one time. It telescopes what might take several sessions to achieve. The tape can be started from the beginning each time.

It should be remembered that we are concerned here only with fluency, and attention to meaning has become secondary. The balance can be restored by reading together the whole book or story from which the passage is taken.

Children often find that the most difficult part of a work sheet is the instructions. If you tape the instructions, the child can work more independently.

> For example:

> On page 4 of 'Adventure by the Sea', find these words and write them down ...'...

> On page 7, find the sentence beginning " But Sandy had lost..." and write down the other three words that end the sentence.

> Look at the sentence written on the card.Underline these words... Copy these words...

> (For the reader at the beginning of Stage 2 see the case example of William, page 72.)

In very small portions, the phonic drills and spelling tests in later chapters can also be taped. If self-checking procedures are incorporated, the child can record his own progress towards mastery by giving himself a score for each completed 'test'.

Computer programs

The microcomputer seems at first sight the ideal medium for drill and practice learning. As a 'teacher' it has great charisma. It is patient, impartial, consistent and tireless. Children are eager to use computers, but at the time of writing they are not as widely used in classrooms as they should be. It may be that early programs did not live up to their promise or, more likely, that the shortage of resources and teacher time has had the effect of limiting their use. But software is increasing and improving all the time, and teachers and the children themselves are becoming sophisticated in using and adapting programs. Because they are constantly being updated, we do not offer lists of recommended programs, evaluations of which are available from the Northwest SEMERC (For contact address see page198). Instead, the following general observations are intended to guide you in selecting and devising programs for children with reading and writing difficulties:

- At present, some of the best uses of the computer are in group work with programs which involve discussion, decision making and problem solving. It is important that children with learning difficulties have full opportunity to participate in these groups and that they are not restricted only to 'drill and practice'. For the purpose of this manual, however, we shall consider only programs designed for individual needs.

- Tasks involving repetitive practice are usually individual and can have the effect of making the child feel isolated. Periods of solo work on the computer may compound this isolation and should therefore be brief.

- Drill and practice programs must be directly related to the child's learning needs. Programs with fixed data are often not suitable. You should be able to alter or enter data, such as the reading vocabulary to be learnt.

- Typing in words on the conventional keyboard may present problems for children. Some programs require the use of only two or three keys, perhaps Return and Space Bar. The fewer the options for the user, however, the more limited the program is likely to be. An increasing number of programs use overlay keyboards with a restricted number of choices. For example, the Sentence Builder (ESM) allows twelve words for sentence making to be entered in the program and the same words to be written on the overlay keyboard. With this the child can make up all possible sentences on the screen, in the same way as wordcards are used in Chapter 5.

- The program's method of marking the child's responses is important. A wrong answer should not produce a more spectacular sound effect than the correct one. Graphics can also distract attention from the learning content, for example, the frog which leaps each time a letter is selected correctly diverts attention from the word to be learnt.

- In learning spelling, the child needs to look at words with intent to memorise the correct sequence of letters in order to learn when they look right. Programs which use Hangman type games, jumbled letters, anagrams or erroneous spellings should be carefully evaluated with this is mind. They do not by themselves enhance the skills of accurate spelling. Another important aspect of spelling is speed and fluency of writing. If children become fairly quick at using the keyboard, speed is not usually a problem, but where every letter correctly keyed in is rewarded, the process of typing a single word can become excessively time-consuming.

- Programs claiming to teach pre-reading skills should be evaluated in terms of what they teach about reading. Learning to remember details of pictures on a screen is unlikely to have any effect on recall of letters in words, or words on a page.

- Programs with good graphics are attractive to children but they may not teach much reading. The words which are easiest to illustrate are nouns, as in *Words-Words-Words*, verbs, as in *Podd* (both ASK software), and adjectives. These are high interest words which children tend to learn most easily any-way from reading books at their own level. The difficult structural words (pronouns, modifiers, auxiliary verbs) are impossible to illustrate and not interesting enough to retain from reading. Programs without graphics are less interesting, but graphics do not support the learning of difficult structural words.

Although computers cannot listen to children read or give immediate prompts in relation to their reading, the use of voice synthesisers has enabled computers to read to or with the children. This has resulted in a number of promising developments. For example, in the Say-That-Again project (Hartas and Moseley, 1993) the Voicecart digital soundcard and software provides opportunities for repeated reading of a challenging text through to the following activities:

- A passage is presented phrase by phrase on the screen with simultaneous computer-produced speech. The pupil can listen to the computer or read 'in chorus' with the computer.

- Pupils read a passage on the screen and have instant access to the audio version which enables them to check their own reading or let the computer read the difficult words for them.

- Pupils can record themselves reading any part of the passage. They get an instant playback, or can switch between their own recording and the original to get an instant comparison.

The equipment in no way replaces the teacher. First, the teacher needs to select and record appropriate texts. Second, when pupils feel confident about reading the chosen passage assisted by the computer, they read the text aloud to the teacher and discuss strategies and options for further practice. The role of the computer is to make the repetitive practice more self-directed and interesting.

The PenDown Talking Computer Program, published by Longman Logotron, prov -ides a second example of recent developments. As a wordprocessor it has the facility of reading out loud the text written by the child. The computer can pronounce each letter (as it is typed), each word (when the child presses the space bar), each sentence, or any combination of the three. It will also read a marked block, or a whole document. Talking PenDown runs on machines already available in many schools, such as Acorn RISC OS.

Projects evaluating Say-That-Again and Talking PenDown report good progress with children whose reading and writing achievements are delayed. The programs seem particularly suitable for older pupils who can direct their own learning. But we need to bear in mind that in both projects the computer and its talking facility are used, not as a supplement to teaching, but as an integral part of comprehensive teaching plans. It is the teaching content which makes the equipment effective.

In our experience considerable emotional and motivational benefits can be derived from 'publishing' children's own work as wordprocessed printouts. The case of Christopher below is typical of children who have regained an interest in reading and writing through dictating stories to a scribe and having the stories collated into a book with a 'published' appearance.

CHRISTOPHER'S OWN BOOK

At the age of eight years Christopher was bored with learning to read and write. Although he enjoyed the content of stories and had plenty to say for himself, he was becoming increasingly reluctant to attempt any tasks which required him to develop accurate and fluent word recognition skills. How could his learning be made more fun? How could the phonics that he needed to learn become more relevant for him? His teacher decided to start by focusing on content through the following activities:

- Christopher dictated his story to the teacher, pausing whenever he wished to talk about it with her. (In this case the teacher was an additional support teacher but it could have been his class teacher, parent or an older pupil).

- To give it status, the story was typed out on a wordprocessor and the printout pasted into his own new book. At this stage Christopher did not need to do any of the writing.

- Christopher read and re-read his own story, at first with the help of his teacher and then to his friends. His friends liked it and he was proud of it. He took it home to read to his parents.

- New stories and other information were gradually added to the book. Some days there was only time to begin a dictation, which was then continued on the next occasion. After additional practice, Christopher willing re-read his own story book to those interested. In this way all the stories continued to be re-read.

- Gradually Christopher, assisted by his teacher, undertook some of the writing himself. She might help him to write words that had by now become familiar to him. Now he also wanted to type out the story for himself.

- It was time to reintroduce the teaching of phonics, following the suggestions in Chapter 7 of this manual. It was an advantage that the example words could be taken from Christopher's own stories. They were words that he was already familiar with and that he wanted to write. For example, the story reproduced below provided many examples of the sound 'ou' such as *Bounty, sound, shout, loud, out*. Christopher and his teacher could now change roles as she dictated known words and short sentences made up of those words to him.

- It can be seen that the main purpose of the wordprocessor was to add glamour to the repetitive teaching, which could have been undertaken without the equipment. Below we reproduce one of the stories dictated by Christopher. The vocabulary and sentence structures of the story are more complex than those that he was usually able to read when following a reading scheme.

The Escape from the Bounty

One night I was playing on my computer and suddenly I found myself on a ship and I soon made a friend and he showed me a room filled with treasure from under the sea. I was very surprised. Just then I heard footsteps and I saw a pirate. He had one eye and his name was Sam. He shouted with a loud gruff voice. "get out". I said. "let's scram. follow me." We both dived under his legs and Sam fell over and Sam was unconscious. Then we ran to the deck and climbed up the crowsnest and then all the pirates came after us. We swam under the Bounty. We climbed up the other side of the Bounty and we stole four bags of gold. two in my hand and two in my friend's hands. We dived back into the sea and the pirates fired cannon balls at us and we saw a ship. It blew up the pirate ship and Bounty and we were saved by the Mary Rose.

SUMMARY

A sense of failure caused by initial difficulties can easily lead to avoidance of reading and writing which, in turn, prevents progress. In this chapter we have considered ways of increasing opportunities for rehearsal and repetition of familiar texts in order to consolidate learning, while retaining the learner's interest and orientation to success Specific teaching suggestions have covered the following areas:

- Prepared reading

- The use of word strips

- Writing and drawing activities

- Additional workbooks and worksheets

- The tape recorder as a medium for repetition

- Computer programs

The case example has illustrated how repetition, including the learning of phonics, can be based on the content of stories that Christopher dictated to his teacher.

Chapter 5

STEP-BY-STEP TEACHING

The purpose of step-by-step teaching is to set very limited learning targets and ensure that the child has really learnt those targets before moving on to new ones. This chapter describes the general principles of the approach in relation to fluent word recognition. The approach is also relevant to the teaching of phonics and spelling described in other chapters of this manual.

INTRODUCTION

The activities described in the previous chapter, Developing Fluency, are based on the assumption that increased opportunities for repetition and success, without very detailed records, is sufficient to ensure progress. But some children, either younger children who have not made a real start in learning to read, or older pupils with more severe difficulties, need an even more exact and repetitive approach. This requires the teacher to set very limited learning targets and ensure that the pupil has thoroughly learnt a particular target task before moving on to the next one. The following case example of William illustrates the approach. The teaching methods are varied, and relevant to other aspects of reading and writing but the learning target itself is specified in a limited measurable form.

WILLIAM: A CASE EXAMPLE

Initial assessment

William was aged six and a half years and had made very little progress in learning the mechanics of reading and writing. His teacher followed the assessments described in Chapter 3 and found that William could just about complete the Stage 1 tasks and was happy to talk about the content of stories. At Stage 2 he had no reliable sight vocabulary and could not read or write any of the single letter sounds. The initial assessment and plan is summarised below.

AN INITIAL ASSESSMENT AND TEACHING PLAN FOR WILLIAM

MEANING

Stage 1: achieved: William likes to hear stories read to him and can predict what might happen next. He understands most of the vocabulary of reading and writing.
Stage 2: not learnt.

PHONICS

Stage 1: William passes the checks of phonemic awareness but not very reliably.
Stage 2: not started.

FLUENCY

Stage 1 learnt: William matches words and letters.
Stage 2 not learnt: William does not recognise words reliably, immediately and fluently.

PLAN OF ACTION

Meaning Stage 2: Continue with assisted reading of as many books as possible noting, whenever appropriate, words and letter sounds which have been covered under the Fluency and Phonics headings of teaching (see Chapter 4).

Fluency Stage 2: A programme of repetitive reading and writing of a limited number of 'sight' words until they have been thoroughly mastered (as described in this chapter).

Phonics Stages 1 and 2: Revise 'I spy' and start systematic practice of initial letter sounds in both reading and writing (see Chapter 7).

The step-by-step approach

In this chapter the step-by-step approach is illustrated through the plans that William's teacher made under the heading of Fluency. Similar step-by-step plans for Phonics will be described in Chapters 6 and 7.

Target objective for William

William's teacher decided to choose twelve frequently used words from the information and stories that he had dictated to her. As an alternative, she could have taken the words from the first pages of an early book in a reading scheme. It was important to select words with different grammatical functions, i.e. **nouns, verbs, prepositions,** so that a variety of sentences could be made up from them (see Table 5.1).The target objective was stated in the following way:

William will read these 12 word cards fluently, unaided and in any order:

I	home	pool
am	Mike	to
going	at	the
swimming	is	big

Table 5.1:
Examples of sentence building

I am swimming
Mike is swimming
I am going swimming
Mike is going swimming
I am at the pool
I am at the big pool
Mike is at the pool
I am going home
Mike is going home
the pool is big
Mike is big
big Mike is going to the big pool
I am big
Continue to make up sentences until
all words have been mastered

Record of progress and criterion of success

The words were listed in William's reading record book. Each word received a tick when William read the word card fluently and without any help. Ten ticks were considered the criterion, i.e. the standard, which indicated that he had mastered the word.

Record keeping as a reward

William was encouraged, with supervision, to match the word cards he had read with those in his record book and to give a tick to the words he had read correctly. He particularly enjoyed counting the ticks each word had received and introduced a competition between the words to see which word was the 'winner' by receiving ten ticks first.

Methods of teaching

- **Sentence building**
  The 12 words were introduced gradually, a few at a time, in an order which enabled short sentences to be made up from them. The sentences were written into a book which became William's 'reading book'. He illustrated his book and read it many times. Table 5.1 gives examples of the kinds of sentences William's teacher wrote. If 'Breakthrough to Literacy' materials had been in use in William's class, his teacher could have helped him to build up the sentence on the Sentence Maker (using only the specified words) before the sentence was copied into William's 'reading book'.

- **Matching identical word cards**
  For example matching 'is' to 'is'. This required two sets of small cards with the words listed above. William was always helped to read the pair of words after matching them.

- **Word recognition**
  The 12 word cards were spread out on the table. William's teacher read out one word at a time and William picked out the word, for example, 'Give me *pool*', 'Give me *big*'.

- **The child tests the teacher**
  The word cards were spread out on the table face up. William read out a word and his teacher had to find it. Sometimes William's teacher made a mistake!

- **Further sentence building**
  The 12 words were each written on several individual cards and stored in a box. William used this 'box of cards' to make up his own sentences.

William's Target Sheet

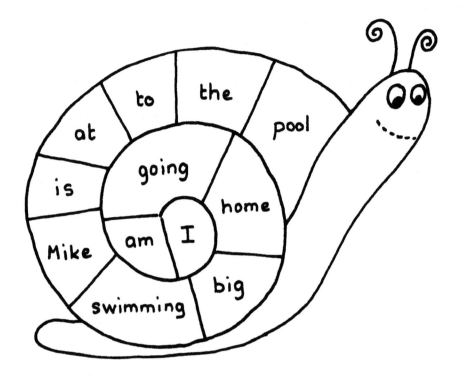

DATE: _____

- **Empty the box game**
  The box of cards from **Further sentence building** was used. William was allowed to remove from the box all the cards he could read. The teacher then helped him with reading the rest of the cards so that the box ended up empty. Later, when William was able to read all the words, he was timed to see how quickly he could empty the box.

- **Further games**
  The 12 words were used for games such as:
  Lotto, where the teacher reads out a card, and William identifies it on his Lotto card;
  Fishing, where players close their eyes to reach for a card behind a screen, and win it if they can read it;
  Pairs, where two sets of the word cards are placed face down on the table and the winner is the one who collects the largest number of pairs.
  Note that in all games visual matching alone was not accepted, and the players always had to read the words aloud.

- **Sentence writing**
  Using the same 12 words, William was helped to write his own sentences. He might, for example, write the initial letter of the word and his teacher would complete the rest. Alternatively, his teacher might start to write the word and William would complete it. The extent to which William could write by himself depended on the parallel developments in his writing skills and initial phonics.

- **Help from parents**
  William often took his teacher-made 'reading book' home and read it to his parents. When William had mastered all the words in the box of cards, he took the box home to show what he had learnt and his parents told him how pleased they were. (William's parents also read many stories to him and with him - see Chapter 2.)

Teaching priorities

With only five minutes a day to spend on individual help for William, his teacher would make sure that each day

- a new sentence was written in his 'reading book';

- William read and wrote the sentence;

- the first set of 12 words was checked over and ticked if read without
  help.

The next target objective

William made good progress and reached the standard, or criterion, of mastery in about two weeks. Now the teacher selected a further set of 12 words and repeated the procedure of sentence building and mastery learning for these words. However, the previously learnt 12 words were also included in the sentence building and sometimes mixed up with the new set of cards. In this way the linguistic content became richer while the previously learnt words continued to be rehearsed. As words were added to William's own 'reading book', the content of the book became more varied and interesting.

N.B. The words could have been taken from the early books of reading schemes. Then, following the suggestions in Chapter 4, William could have read these books in parallel with the sentence building activities. And, as described in the next chapter on phonics, the words that William was using for sentence building could also be used to support his learning of initial letter sounds.

HOW TO PLAN A STEP-BY-STEP PROGRAMME

The case example of William illustrates the procedure of planning a detailed programme. In more general terms, the sequence followed by William's teacher is presented diagrammatically in Table 5.2. To provide an overview of the planning and teaching involved, we discuss below each of the subheadings in Table 5.2.

1. Make an initial assessment

The assessment follows the framework described in Chapters 1 and 3 and summarised in Table 3.1 (page 32). It involves decisions about the *stage* of reading and writing reached by the pupil and his or her relative strengths and weaknesses under the three headings of **Meaning, Fluency** and **Phonics.** The case example of William is presented in this way in at the beginning of this chapter.

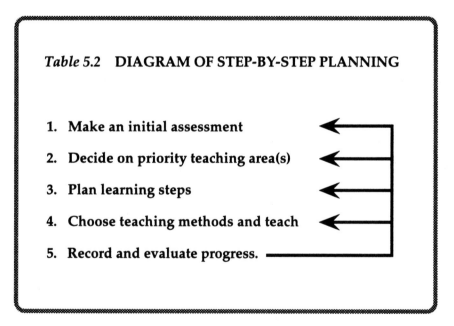

Table 5.2   **DIAGRAM OF STEP-BY-STEP PLANNING**

1. **Make an initial assessment**

2. **Decide on priority teaching area(s)**

3. **Plan learning steps**

4. **Choose teaching methods and teach**

5. **Record and evaluate progress.**

2. Decide on priority teaching area(s)

This is perhaps the most controversial part of the procedure. Which aspect should William's teacher start with? Should she concentrate on building up a bank of sight words, on letter sounds and phonics, or on approaches based on reading with and for the child? Ideally the answer should be all three so that tuition moves on a broad front and takes account of the interaction between linguistic, visual, and phonic information. The ideal plan for William would consist of the following three main elements:

- Assisted reading and writing offering a rich vocabulary and exciting content (see Chapter 2).
- Repetitive reading and writing of a limited number of words as described in this chapter.
- Equally systematic and repetitive practice of initial letter sounds through

'I Spy' games and the illustrated alphabet described in Chapter 6,

With so little time for individual instruction, teachers have to decide which of the elements should receive the highest priority. William's teacher chose to start with the introduction of a limited number of sight words. She could have chosen to start with phonics or to use the sight words as illustrations of the phonics she was teaching (see page 98). The teacher's task was made easier because William' parents were keen to help and were able to read to and with him in ways described in Chapter 2.

The class teacher in charge of some 30 children has usually time to make only a 'five minute' plan for the pupil with difficulties. It therefore becomes particularly important to decide on the highest priority for that pupil and to stick to the priority teaching area for long enough to enable the child with learning difficulties to make progress.

When a child struggles with reading, it is tempting to switch from one task to another in the hope that something else will work better. This can result in an approach described as 'a little of a lot' where the child is not given enough time to learn any one task. Children with learning difficulties need more time to practise the same objective until it is properly learnt. Provided that the initial assessment is reasonably accurate, children will progress when they have the chance to practise a specified task for a sufficiently long period of time; in other words, when they have an opportunity to learn 'a lot of a little'.

But this approach does have pitfalls. When the learning task has been narrowed down to only one specific area, the danger is that the overall picture of the nature of reading may be neglected. If, for example, the teacher concentrates on a limited set of words then she may be tempted to keep on adding to the list of sight words and to neglect to ensure that other aspects in turn receive intensive emphasis. Similarly, if letter sounds and phonics are taken as the priority area, it is important to arrange practice in such a way that the words exemplifying phonic regularities become part of the pupil's automatic reading and writing vocabulary. And all along the teacher must remember that the main purpose of teaching is to help the pupil to enjoy and understand the meaning of the text. The sight words and phonics must, therefore, be encountered again in the context of 'real' reading of stories and other information and in the children's own writing.

It can be seen that getting the balance right is not easy. Although the teacher is guided by her initial assessment of the pupil's strengths and weaknesses, in the end she has to make the decision herself about priorities, and the ways of ensuring that all aspects of reading and writing are included.

3. Plan learning steps

Having decided which aspect is to receive concentrated practice, the teacher next considers ways of subdividing the task into sufficiently small learning steps. In the case example of William, his teacher chose the words to be included in the initial set of 12 words, and the order of introducing them. These decisions were based on her judgement and knowledge of William. She could have chosen a different set of words or a smaller or larger number of words. Initial decisions remain to some extent arbitrary and only records of progress will indicate whether the teacher was right. If the child is not progressing, the clearly specified learning target forms a starting point for subdividing the task into still smaller steps or for considering alternative methods or priorities.

As was discussed in Chapter 1, literacy is a great deal more than the sum of particular sub-skills. Nevertheless, the step-by-step approach does assume that certain aspects can be practised and learnt as skills. It is useful to think of the learning of skills in terms of a five-stage hierarchy as described by Haring *et al*, (1978). The learning hierarchy is presented in Table 5.3.

Table 5.3

LEARNING A NEW SKILL

Acquisition: The pupil begins to learn the skill and is starting to do it accurately.

Fluency: The pupil performs the skill accurately and fluently.

Maintenance: The pupil continues to perform fluently over a long period of time without any teacher assistance.

Generalisation: The pupil can apply the new skill to different tasks following instruction.

Adaptation: The pupil applies the new skill in new settings without any instruction.

In the case example of William, the learning steps were arranged in a cumulative way so that words learned earlier were incorporated in later sentence building with a further set of new words. This ensured that the requirements of the first three headings in Table 5.3 were met, i.e., a set of sight words received intensive practice until they were read fluently and without hesitation, and then the same words were deliberately included in further activities to maintain the learning. Another important reason for including the 'old' words in further practice was to make the sentence building activities more interesting and linguistically relevant.

The last two headings in Table 5.3, **generalisation** and **adaptation,** remind us of the limitations of instruction when it is not transferred to a variety of other situations. Until William reads the words he has learnt in a selection of books, with and without direct help from teachers and parents, we cannot be sure that he has really mastered what we have taught him. This is why it is essential to complement specific learning of this kind with assisted reading of as many books as possible. The teacher can then ensure that the pupil uses newly learnt skills in many contexts. She can keep a check on his use of these skills by having at hand the record book listing the sight words and phonics mastered and, if necessary, helping the pupil to refer to it as to a dictionary when the words are encountered in a new story.

4. Choose teaching methods and teach

William's teacher introduced a variety of methods for teaching the 12 specified sight words. By this means William did not become bored by the limited task and his motivation was enhanced both by his success and by the part he played in helping his teacher to record the progress. All the teaching methods were planned in such a way that William could complete his assignments successfully. For example, his teacher made sure that William attained reasonably high 'scores' when words were checked over, and if he could not read a word or if he made a mistake, his teacher would help him to read the word, using encouraging prompts such as 'Let's try again' and avoiding comments such as 'No, that's wrong!'.

The choice of methods depends on teacher preference and the circumstances of teaching such as the amount of time available for instruction and the extent to which practice can take place within the ordinary classroom alongside other class or group activities. If parents or other helpers are involved, it is possible to introduce a wider range of methods. There are no hard and fast rules about methods of teaching as long as the pupil feels successful and as long as there is progress. While the selection of methods in this manual should provide a good starting point, teachers will be able to devise their own games and activities for increasing repetition of a basic vocabulary.

5. Record and evaluate progress

It can be difficult to determine the criterion, or standard, of success required to show that the pupil has really learnt the task and, again, the decision has to be left to teacher judgement and knowledge of the individual pupil. How many times will the child have to give the correct response and how quick and fluent should the response be before it is felt that a particular objective has been learnt? William's teacher chose as her criterion ten 'ticks' for each sight word but she could have chosen a different criterion or she could have changed it in the light of her observations when teaching William. If the standard set by the teacher is too high then time can be wasted in unnecessary repetition and, if it is too low, then the pupil will not have had the opportunity to master the task thoroughly. The individual teacher will, however, refine her ability to set appropriate targets and criteria by establishing a record-keeping system which checks at a later date whether the learnt task has still been retained. This form of record keeping requires a longer-term plan for each objective. Three items are required:

(a)   The date when practice began on a particular target task.

(b)   The date the task was mastered, i.e. the criterion of success was achieved. This may be the same day, a few days later or a week later, but too long spent on one objective usually indicates that it is too difficult and that a modification is necessary.

(c)   The date a check was made on continuing mastery of the task. This may be a few days later, one week later or a month later. The time interval is not crucial as long as a system of checking that the skill or knowledge has been retained is built into the record-keeping system. If not retained, **re-learning becomes necessary** but this is usually done in a much shorter time than the original learning.

It is tempting merely to tick objectives as they are mastered. This takes up just as much time but conveys far less information than a date. For example, the time-lapse between beginning the learning of a task and its mastery gives the teacher an indication of the rate at which the pupil is learning and shows whether the pupil can cope with larger or smaller learning steps. It is also useful to provide a space in the record-keeping system for notes on methods used, including any changes in method or materials. In Table 5.4 below we have again used the case example of William to illustrate one format of this type of record keeping.

Table 5.4:

WILLIAM'S READING RECORD

Standard: *10 'ticks' for each word = mastered*

Words to learn	Record with dates			Comments
	Practising	**Mastered**	**Checked**	
I am going swimming Mike is at pool to the big				
etc. further words				

It is now possible to evaluate whether the child is making progress with the target task. If progress is good, the teacher will move to the next set of words in the programme. If the target is still not being attained, a re-examination of the diagram in Table 5.2 will indicate what action can be taken. The arrows in the diagram point to the aspects which may need to be thought about again:

(a)   Look at your assessment again to see whether your initial assessment was correct.

(b)   Consider whether there are more appropriate priority teaching areas.

(c)   Think of more interesting learning materials or smaller learning steps.

(d)   Reconsider teaching methods and ways of enhancing interest.

SUMMARY

This chapter has made use of the case example of William to outline the planning and recording involved in step-by-step approaches to learning difficulties. It has also demonstrated what we mean by the expression **interactive assessment and teaching** where initial assessments lead to plans which are adjusted in the light of the child's response to the teaching.

Later chapters in the manual provide further examples of teaching sequences and methods of record keeping. When following a step-by-step teaching approach, it is important not to lose sight of other aspects of literacy, in particular those which belong to the **meaning** heading in Figure 1.1.

Chapter 6

PHONICS AT STAGES 1 AND 2

Detailed teaching suggestions in this chapter cover the following areas:

STAGE 1
- **Rhymes and rhyming words**
- **Auditory sound blending**
- **Auditory recognition of initial letter sounds ('I Spy')**

STAGE 2
- **Reading and writing initial letter sounds**
- **Reading and writing c-v-c words (e.g. hat, sun)**

INTRODUCTION

The teaching of phonics draws deliberate attention to regular correspondences between spoken sounds and their written representations. Stage 1 in this manual is concerned with the pre-requisite developments in phonological awareness while Stage 2 starts to link these auditory achievements with their written visual forms.

Children who have had the opportunity to enjoy nursery rhymes and word games may come to school ready to start at Stage 2. Other children may need carefully planned help in order to learn to perceive rhyme and the initial sounds in words. They begin at Stage 1.

At Stage 2 also, many children progress remarkably easily. As they learn to represent spoken sounds in writing, they start to work out the 'rules' for themselves. For example, having written the word 'hat' they may, by analogy, recognise or write other words with the same spelling pattern such as 'mat'. The analytical method of teaching phonics helps the child to make these inferences.

Children who experience difficulty in learning to read and write may not be able to take advantage of the analytical method of teaching. Their memory for linking visual and auditory symbols may not be sufficient to retain a given written symbol and the sound it represents in the context of the whole word. As a consequence, on seeing unfamiliar words with the same spelling pattern, they cannot use the analogy because they are not able to remember what sound the spelling pattern represents. These children may need a more direct and repetitive method of learning phonics.

Synthetic phonic methods start from single letters and common letter combinations. Words are built up or synthesised from their elements (e.g. b-at, sp-oo-n, ch-ur-ch, scr-ap, ex-ten-sion). Rules are taught and practised, not deduced.

It is not necessary to teach every possible letter combination but only the most commonly used ones. These are listed on page 127 at the end of Chapter 7. After that, pupils can often work out further 'rules' for themselves in the context of reading and writing. In other words, they may now be ready for the more natural analytical forms of learning.

Language and general knowledge cues help the reader predict new words from context and from their initial letters. If the child does not use context cues, we can help by re-reading the sentence for her and stopping at the unknown word, for example: 'She drank a glass of m... – what do you think she drank?'

If a pupil needs to be taught phonics in a detailed and repetitive manner, it is particularly important to ensure that any possible hearing loss has been identified. It is not uncommon for children to have a fluctuating hearing loss associated with catarrhal blockage or, in a few cases, an unidentified sensory-neural hearing loss may account for the child's inability to discriminate between letter sounds which are within a certain frequency range. If you have any doubts about the child's ability to hear well, arrange for her to see the school's Clinical Medical Officer or ask the parents to take the child to their family doctor.

STAGE 1: EARLY DEVELOPMENT

A. RHYMES AND NON-RHYMES

The following activities are suitable for children who

- did not cope with the rhyme detection task described on page 35 in Chapter 3.

- need further consolidation before you are sure that they hear rhyme easily and consistently.

Silly nursery rhymes

Choose a familiar rhyme written in rhyming couplets. Alter the second rhyme to another non-rhyming word. If the child knows the rhyme, she will correct you triumphantly! For example:

'Little Miss Muffett
sat on a chair'

'Hickory Dickory dock
the mouse ran up the hill'

Continue along the following lines:

Yes, it's Clock: Hickory Dickory Dock, the mouse ran up the .....   Clock/Dock
sound alike don't they? Do you know Jack and Jill went   up the .... Yes, Jill/hill
sound alike. Can you tell me another word that sounds like hill?
What about these words: mill? pill? fill? table?

Other suitable verses are Ding Dong Bell, Mary Mary, Humpty Dumpty, Diddle Diddle Dumpling. This is a good game for children and parents to enjoy but it assumes that children have already learnt about nursery rhymes at home. Sometimes we have also found that children think so intensively about the content of the rhymes that they are not listening to the rhyme itself.

Picture Pairs and Rhyming Snap

Present pictures of pairs of objects. The child names the pictures and collects pairs that rhyme. Before beginning, check on names and pronunciation, especially if the child speaks with a regional dialect or has difficulties with speech articulation.

The pictures can also be used to for games of Snap or Pelmanism.
A selection of suitable pictures is provided on page 100 at the end of this chapter.

Find the odd-one-out

Present sets of pictures in arrays of three or four, each with one non-rhyming 'odd-one-out', which the child is asked to identify. A selection of pictures is provided at the end of this chapter (page 100).

Picture Pairs and Rhyming Snap

Find the Odd One Out

Rhyming riddles

This is an oral game which may also be played with a group of children at school or by parents and child at home. The child supplies the final rhyming word in each couplet. For example:

> Sammy Cox put on his ...socks.
> Mrs Mill paid the ...bill.
> Little Ben writes with a ...pen.
> Uncle Paul is very ...tall.
> In my house there is a ...mouse.

Note that all these rhyming games are purely oral and no reading is involved. There is therefore no need to confine words to easy phonic patterns.

B. AUDITORY SOUND BLENDING

If the child did not cope with the task of auditory sound blending on page 35 in Chapter 3, more practice will be needed in this area. The task may have been unfamiliar to the child and you may find that, after some further instruction, she understands what is required and is then able to blend the segments of the words quite well.

The words are not presented in a written form to the child; the teacher says the sounds pausing for less than a second between each sound segment and the child then says the whole word.

When teaching the child to blend the segments of the word, it is better to start with longer words which are divided into big 'chunks' than short words where segments consist of individual letter sounds. For example, the child is likely to find *lemon-ade* easier than *st-op*. We have listed some of common longer words in Table 6.1 which you can use as a start for teaching sound blending.

Sometimes children can have difficulty with sound discrimination and blending because they are not attending well. In other words, they have not learnt to listen carefully. To help the child, ask her to sit opposite you and to look carefully at your mouth as you say the segments of the word. (Note the importance of making sure that the child's hearing has been checked.)

If the child continues to have difficulty with sound blending, you will have to shorten the one second pause between the segments of the word so that the segments nearly merge together as you say them. Always help the child complete the word successfully even if you are virtually saying the word for her first. When the child is able to merge the word segments, you can gradually lengthen your pauses again until the child can blend the segments into one word when you again pause for about one second between them.

Table 6.1 **SOUND BLENDING**

aero - plane	chim - pan - zee
break - fast	hand - ker - chief
bed - room	beau - ti - ful
after - noon	im - por - tant
play - ground	mo - tor - bike
lemon - ade	hos - pi - tal
adven - ture	pho - to - graph
car - pet	un - der - stand
seven - teen	te - le - phone
cheer - ful	mar - ma - lade
cur - tain	yes - ter - day

It is not necessary to labour with the sound blending tasks for too long. If the child continues to have difficulty when you repeat the test on page 35 after some teaching, note this in your records and move on. There may be further difficulty when the child comes to Stage 2 and is required to blend sounds represented by written symbols (e.g. h-at). You may then wish to return to this earlier stage of sound blending. You will also anticipate that the child needs much repetition in order to learn to blend combinations of letter sounds into words. An approach which starts with known sightwords, as described on page 98, may be of help here.

C. AUDITORY RECOGNITION OF INITIAL LETTER SOUNDS ('I SPY')

If the pupil did not pass the 'I Spy' test described in Chapter 3 page 36, he will need extra help in learning to 'hear' the first sound of the spoken word. The following games, suggested by Muriel Bridge, are designed to help develop this ability. They may be played with the individual child or a small group of two or three pupils. Only initial letter sounds are used, not the alphabetical names of the letters.

N.B. The games described use toy objects. If you have difficulty obtaining the objects, pictures may be used instead. Page 103 at the end of this chapter contains a small selection of suitable pictures.

Easy Kim's Game

A tray of four objects is assembled, each of which begins with the same sound, e.g. saucer, sock, spoon, salt. The child is asked to name each object. The teacher repeats each name (correcting if necessary), but slightly emphasising the first sound by sustaining it: 'sssaucer', 'sssock', etc. The child repeats this. When all the objects have been named in this way, he is asked which sound they all start with. The teacher may need to rephrase the question several times and repeat the naming of the objects, overemphasising the initial sound even more. In a few cases the teacher may have to tell the child what the initial sound is. When this happens, the procedure will have to be repeated, possibly on several further occasions. The tray of objects is called the 'sssss tray'.

The teacher has some reserve objects which may or may not begin with sss. The child examines and names each object and is helped to exaggerate the first sound to determine whether it belongs to the 'sssss tray' or not. Other items could include: sweets, scissors, stone, seeds. It is important to select the non-s items carefully. Avoid similar sounds, such as sh, and choose a strong contrast, such as m. Sustainable sounds are easier to 'hear': a,e,f,h,i,l,m,n,o,r,s,v.

For the purpose of the usual Kim's Game, the 'ssss tray' is covered over and the child tries to recall all the objects on the tray.

Easy Clue Game

Once the child can 'hear' the initial s sound in the way suggested above, she can play the Clue Game. The teacher says: 'It begins with "sssss" and it is ...' (e.g. a boy's name, a girl's name, an animal, in the sky, where you wash up in the kitchen).

The easy Kim's Game and the easy Clue Game can be repeated for different initial letter sounds. Do this only for a small selection of initial letters. Once the child has got the idea and completes the task with ease, she is ready for the next games.

The Home Game

The following games involve discrimination between two or more sounds.

-The pupil allocates each object from a jumbled assortment to its proper HOME: the 'ssss tray' or the 'mmmm tray', etc. He is encouraged to name each object, exaggerating the first sound to decide which is the correct HOME.

-The teacher prepares two trays of objects chosen by initial sound but two objects are in the wrong HOME. The pupil must find which objects are in the wrong HOME and return them to the correct one.

The game can be extended by introducing a third or fourth tray.

Guess Which One

Once four different sounds have been isolated in this way, the teacher presents a group of four objects, one for each sound. The pupil is asked to pick up or point at the object for which the teacher has given the first sound.

Hard Kim's Game

Cover the tray of four objects (each beginning with a different sound). The teacher asks: 'Can you remember what was on the tray beginning with ...?' The difficulty of this task can be increased by adding more objects to the tray.

Another version of this game is for the teacher to ask: "Is there something on the tray beginning with ...?' Make sure the answer is not always 'yes'.

When the child is able to play the normal game of 'I Spy', you can test her using the task described on page 36 in Chapter 3. If the test is passed the child is ready to learn the written representations of the letter sounds as described in Stage 2.

STAGE 2: BEGINNING TO READ AND WRITE INDEPENDENTLY

A. SINGLE LETTER SOUNDS

Having learnt to 'hear' the first sound of a word in the 'I Spy' game and through the activities described in the previous pages, the child is ready to move on to recognising the written representations of the letter sounds. If the child already knows many of the written letter sounds, the test on page 40 (Chapter 3) will help you identify which letters have not been learnt. The teaching sequences described below assume that the child is starting from the beginning.

Where to start

Select no more than three unknown letters of distinctive and contrasting shape and sound (e.g. s,m,a). The beginning reader will find it easier to learn sustainable sounds (e.g. m,f,s,n) rather than sounds which can be pronounced only briefly (e.g. b,c,t).

The illustrated letter cards: A set of photocopyable cards is provided on page 108.

The child gradually builds up his own individual pack of letter cards, starting with the first three unknown letters. Each card in the pack has on one side the letter and a picture of an object which begins with that letter. On the reverse side of the card, only the letter is shown. This is illustrated overleaf:

Picture side   Reverse side

Children often like to select their own 'clue' object for a given letter and to draw the object for themselves on the picture side of the card. Those who are not good at drawing may prefer to make the choice of object and to have the teacher draw it. There are commercially produced pictures which can be used for this purpose. We have included at the end of this chapter a set of alphabet cards. These cards can be reproduced so that the child has his or her own individual set.

Teaching methods: picture side up

(a)   Select the first three letter cards to be learnt (e.g. m,s,a).

(b)   Place the cards picture side up on the table.

(c)   Point at the a card and say 'a - apple'; the child repeats 'a - apple'.
        Point at the s card and say 's - snake'; the child repeats 's - snake'.
        Point at the m card and say 'm - milk';the child repeats 'm - milk'.

(d)   Sustain the sound (e.g. mmm) and ask the child to point at the right card. Repeat this for the other two cards. Continue in random order for all three cards until the child always points to the right card easily and quickly.

(e)   Now point to each letter card and ask the child to make the correct sound. Repeat until the child's responses are fluent.

(f)   Follow the same procedure with three more cards.

(g)   You now have a pack of six cards. Select any three cards at random and check whether the child can still recall the sounds with ease (with the picture side up so that the mnemonic clue is easily available).

(h)   Continue to add cards to the pack in this way (only using the picture side of the cards) and repeat the activity daily for a few minutes over a period of a week or more.

(i)   The child will learn to respond with increasing speed to each card until you   are able to flick through the pack of cards and the child's response to the letter/picture clue has become instant.

Teaching methods: the 'quick flip'

(a)   The child is now ready to learn to recognise letters without their picture clues. Start again with the three original cards.

(b)   Place the cards picture side down on the table so that the child can only see the letter on the reverse side of the card.

(c)   Ask the child to say the correct sound for each letter. If he cannot recall the sound, allow him to make a 'quick flip', i.e. take a very quick look at the picture side of the card. Having seen the picture clue, the child is able to give the correct sound. Continue to rehearse this until the three cards require no more 'quick flips'. The child may need several days of practice before he can automatically give the right sound without reference to the picture clue.

(d)   Gradually add more cards to the pack, always continuing to revise previously learnt cards.

(e)   The child will often develop 'x-ray eyes' visualising the clue picture on the other side of the card and so remembering it by heart. As he becomes more proficient, you can gradually increase the speed of the child's response to each card. Eventually he will be able to flick through the whole pack of cards saying each letter sound instantly.

You may prefer to introduce the 'quick flip' much earlier in the procedure, for example, after the first three letters with picture clues have been learnt. The teaching method then consists of alternating between learning initial letters with picture clues and practising automatic recognition of single letters without picture clues.

Extra games for reinforcement

(a)   Another version of 'I Spy': The teacher says, 'I Spy ...something beginning with ...' but instead of saying the letter sound, she shows a letter card or writes the letter.

(b)   Games such as Pairs, Snap or Happy Families can be played by making further sets of letter cards. It is essential that pupils always say the letter sound aloud when pairing up the cards so that they do not succeed with the task on the basis of visual matching alone.

The multisensory approach

It can be helpful to introduce the writing of the letter sounds at an early stage. In the multisensory approach the children trace over the written representations of the letters saying the sound as they do the tracing. Later they repeatedly write the sound while simultaneously again saying it. In this way the child can see, hear and feel the handmovements involved in writing the letter so that reading, spelling and handwriting become mutually reinforcing activities.

Dictation

The child should be able to read and write the letter sounds before we can be sure that they have really been learnt. Dictation can be started as soon as the first letters of the illustrated alphabet have been introduced. The task can be too demanding for the younger child and the teacher may decide to introduce the written work at a later stage, for example, when the child has learnt to recognise most letter sounds. Once the child can form the letters correctly, we want her to be able to write them from memory. We can dictate the letter sounds in random order or dictate a list of interesting words for which the child writes the first letter only. The task of learning to write letter sounds from dictation can also be divided into smaller learning steps.

Using letter knowledge when reading

The transfer of letter recognition from the set of cards to reading books and other information does not always happen automatically. As soon as the child has learnt a few letter sounds, the teacher can scan ahead to locate a word beginning with one of the newly learnt letters. The word should occur towards the end of a phrase or sentence so that there are enough meaningful cues based on context. The teacher covers up the word except for the first letter. The pupil is encouraged to 'guess' from preceding meaning and the initial letter. Records of the child's progress will indicate which letter sounds can be treated in this way. With practice over a period of time, the child should, at this stage, acquire the habit of speedy integration of cues based on context and initial letters.

B. INTRODUCING WORD BUILDING

Before starting, ensure that the child can play 'I Spy', can identify single letter sounds and use those sounds as initial letter cues when reading. When introducing word building skills, we should continue to encourage the use of context and word meaning so that the pupil does not learn to rely on 'sounding out' the entire word as her only strategy.

How should word building be taught?

There are two somewhat contrasting views about how words should be split up at this stage. We have called them **Method A and Method B.**

Method A concludes that children perceive words as initial sounds and 'the rest' (i.e. 'onset' and 'rime'). This would imply that word blending is taught as :

> h-at
> p-at
> s-at   etc

Method B emphasises the distortions involved in pronouncing consonants in isolation. When attempting to say h-at or p-at we actually say huh-at or puh-at. This makes it harder for children to hear the blend. The suggestion is then that blending should be taught as:

> ha-t
> pa-t
> sa-t   etc.

Both arguments are defensible. The method chosen will depend on the preferences of the teacher and the way the individual child learns best. We suggest, therefore, that you try out both ways to find out which seems the better for the child concerned.

Materials: You will need commercially produced plastic or wooden cut-out letters or letters written individually on fairly small cards (e.g. 2cm x 2cm).

Method A learning sequence:

(a)   Make up the word 'at' with the letter cards and help the child read it.
Now select initial consonant letters m,p,c,b,f,s,r to make up words and
practise until the child reads the words easily and fluently in any order.
For example:

> m-at
> p-at
> r-at   etc

(b) Make up some different short two letter combinations such as 'in', 'it', 'on', 'up', 'ed', 'an'. Focus on one of them at a time and help the child read it. Select again initial consonant letters to make up three letter words. The child reads each combination in turn and identifies those combinations which, when blended, make up a 'real' word, e.g.

> p-in
> b-in
> f-in
> t-in

Method B learning sequence:

(a) Select a vowel *'a'* along with the consonants t,m,p,c,b,f,s,r,g. Place the consonant cards (or plastic letters) on the table underneath each other. Move the *'a'* card to the side of each consonant in turn and blend together the consonant and vowel. For example:

> p - a   -   pa
> c - a   -   ca
> m - a   -   ma

Continue to blend until the child can say without any hesitation or pause between the two sounds: pa, ca, ma, fa, sa, etc. It may take several sessions for the child's response to become so easy and automatic that there is no need for prior demonstration.

(b) Introduce final consonants t,n,g,p,d.

> Blend
> pa - t   -   pat
> ca - n   -   can
> ma - p   -   map   etc

This step should follow easily from the previous one. Repeat in random order until the child's responses are fluent. It can take several sessions.

Method A and Method B learning sequences continued:

(c) Let the child make her own words by arranging the letters thus:

> p   s
> c   t
> m   a   n
> s   g
> f   m

Take one consonant to blend with a. Add the third letter from the final column. Make sure that the initial consonant and the vowel are as far as possible pronounced as one unit. Practise until the child is able to blend quite fluently.

(d) Step (c) can be consolidated through writing. The child writes her own words and later reads them out to the teacher.

(e) Continue steps (a) to (d) with each vowel in turn

(f) Once all the above steps have been mastered, introduce the 'sound dictionary'. Draw five columns on a sheet of paper headed by each of the vowels: a,e,i,o,u. Dictate three letter words with the short vowel, e.g. 'map', 'let', 'cup', 'hot', 'six'. Lists of example words are provided on page 126 at the end of Chapter 7. The child repeats the dictated word aloud and listens carefully. She then identifies the vowel in each word, finds the appropriate column on the 'sound dictionary' sheet and writes the word. A few children may confuse similar sounds such as *e* and *i* or *o* and *u*. Encourage the child to look closely at you as you pronounce the word and to attend to the 'feel' of the word in his mouth as he repeats it. If the confusion persists, note this in your records and move on to the next stage. When reading a meaningful text the child should be able to compensate for this weakness through contextual cues.

(g) The child is now ready to write simple sentences from dictation. For example:

> 'The cat and the dog sat on the mat'
> 'He had a pan with a lid'
> 'It is fun to sit in the sun'

Whenever possible, use words from the child's own reading as this will help her transfer what she has learnt to more independent reading. When the child can read and spell the short sentences, she will have acquired the concept of written language as a sequence of letter sounds which merge to make distinct and meaningful words.

(h) The use of the 'sound dictionary' and dictation can now be extended to phonics at the Stage 3 level if required. By introducing initial and final consonant blends and digraphs, we can build up an extensive reading vocabulary based on the short medial vowel (e.g. 'shop', 'trick', 'lamp', 'brush', 'spend' - see the next chapter).

Using known sight words as a basis for word building

A few children may remain unable to blend single sounds into short words despite carefully structured teaching. Such children might respond to the approach tried by Glyn's teacher.

Glyn had a sight vocabulary which included the phonically regular words 'red', 'pig', 'cat', 'hen'. Although he could read these words, he could not read new words consisting of the same consonant - vowel - consonant structures. He could identify most single letters by their sound and was just becoming adept at 'I Spy'. His teacher used 'cat' as a starting point in the following way:

(a)　　Can you tell me this word? (cat)
(b)　　Listen to the sounds in 'cat' - c-a-t
(c)　　Now you say it
(d)　　Let's say it like this: c-a-t - c-ca-cat
(e)　　Say it after me
(f)　　Point to the letters in 'cat' as I say them
(g)　　You say the letters and see if I can point to them
(h)　　Now guess which word on the page I am saying: h-e-n
(g)　　Use each of the known sight words in this way.

By alternating between well-known sight words and their constituent sounds, the teacher enabled Glyn to grasp the concept of phonic blending. This method can also be useful for children who have difficulty in distinguishing between short vowel sounds. Sight words containing the target vowel become key words for reading or writing new short vowel words. Reading schemes which contain a reasonable number of consonant-vowel-consonant words are suitable for this purpose.

RECORD KEEPING

Each of the teaching sequences in this chapter can be recorded in the way described in Chapter 5, i.e. by defining steps in the form of learning targets, by setting a standard of performance to indicate when the target has been mastered, and by recording progress with dates under the headings of Working on, Mastered, Checked. This format is illustrated in Table 6.2 with reference to the sequence for introducing word building on page 95. To allow more spaces for recording, teachers may find it easier to turn the paper so that the longest side is in a horizontal position. But you need not necessarily follow this format at all. It is the checking of whether the child has really mastered a learning task that matters and not the exact format that the record sheet takes.

Table 6.2 A RECORD OF C-V-C WORD RECOGNITION

Learning targets	Record with dates			Comments
	Practising	Mastered	Checked	
pat, can, map man, sat, pan cat, fan, fat				
pen, net, red, leg, pet, hen, set, men, let				
pot, dog, top, fog, hot, got, job, not, hop				
pig, tin, big, fit, bin, sit, win, bit, bin				
bus, cup, run, sun, cut, hug, bun, but, hut				
The 'sound dictionary' see page 97 for instructions				
Words from the above targets read and written in any order				
The child can write short sentences from dictation e.g.'It is fun to sit in the sun'.				
Further targets can be added at Stage 3 (next chapter) which include such words as stop, step, fist, stick				

Standard for 'mastered': words read or written correctly and fluently in any order

Pictorial Illustrations for the games
of

Picture Pairs
Rhyming Snap
Find the Odd-One-Out

Instructions for playing the games can be found on
pages 85-88

**The pictures fall into the following rhyming
groups:**

bat	sun	wall	house	frog
hat	bun	ball	mouse	log
cat	gun			
bee	ring	pan	tap	cake
tree	king	man	rap	rake
key		van		
sock	book	star	moon	hen
lock	hook	car	spoon	pen
				ten

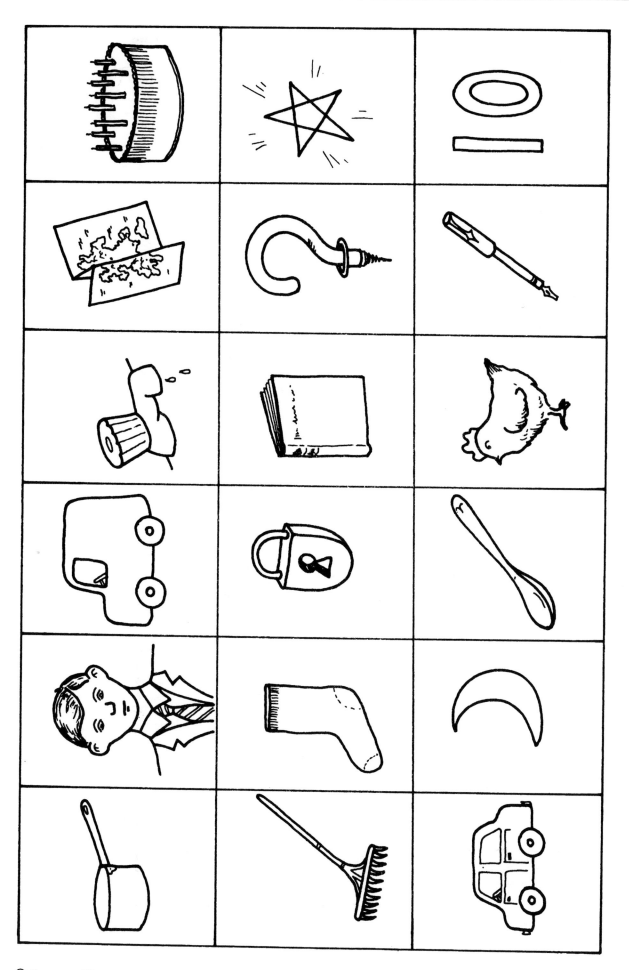

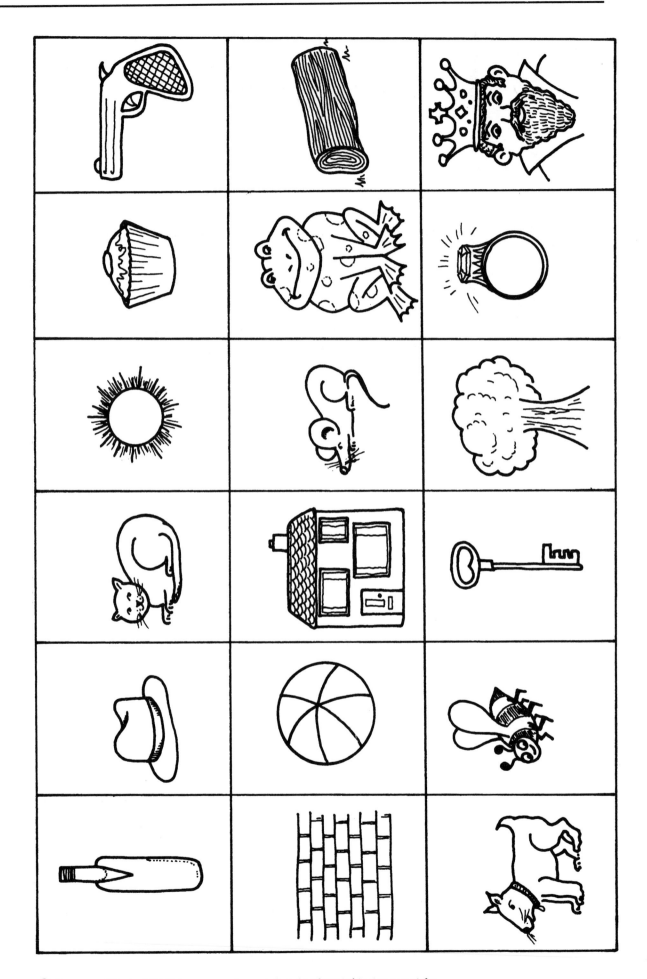

PICTURES FOR INITIAL LETTER GAMES

The following pictures are for the games described under the heading 'Auditory Recognition of Initial Letter Sounds' – (I Spy') described on pages 89:

Easy Kim's game
Easy Clue game
The Home game
Guess Which One
Hard Kim's Game

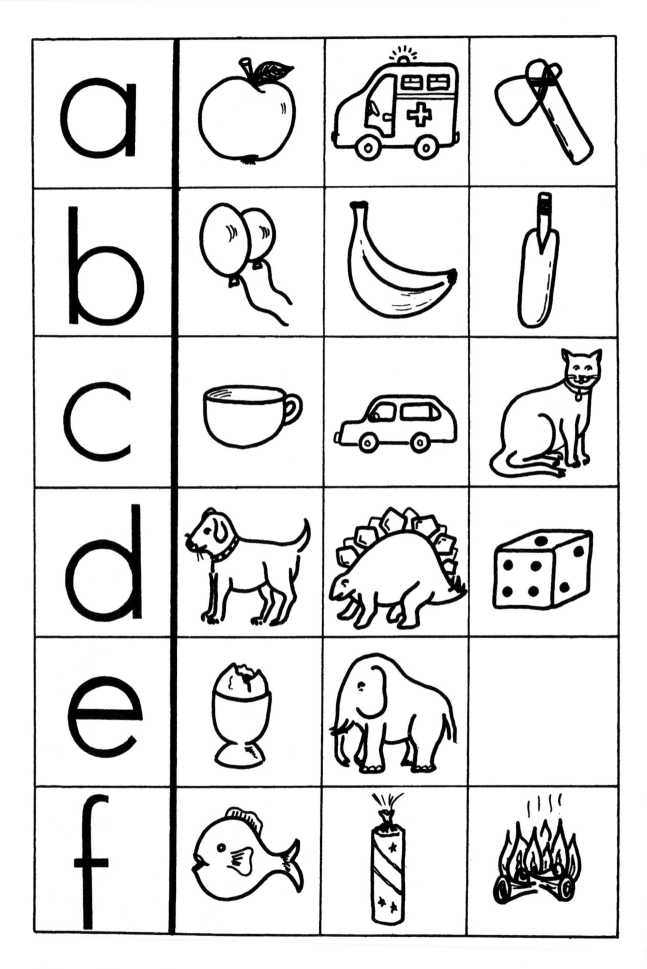

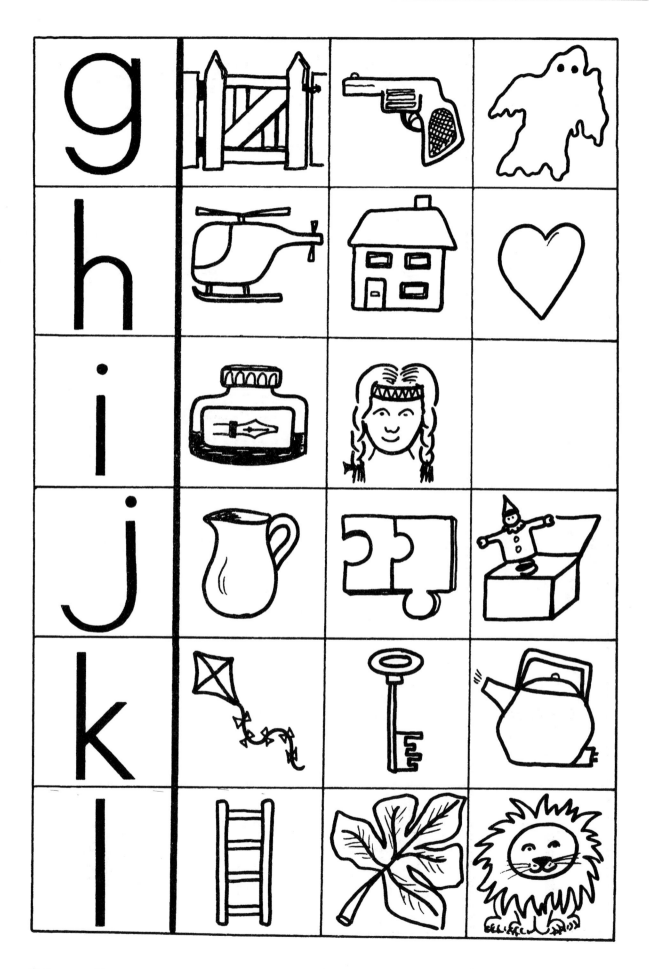

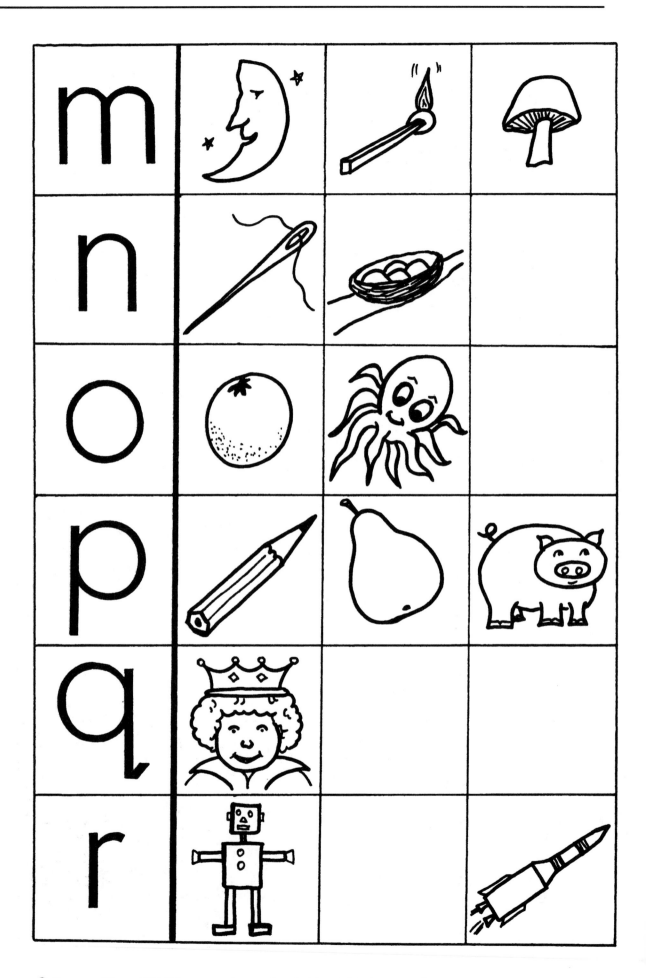

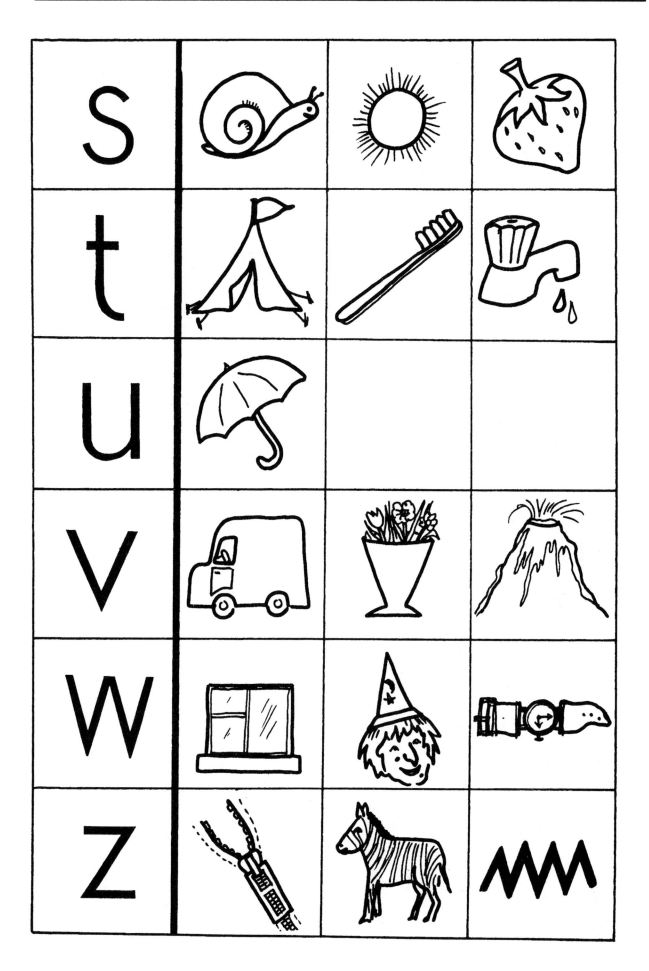

ILLUSTRATED LETTER CARDS

This chapter has described activities and games which help children acquire early competencies in phonological awareness and letter recognition. The illustrated letter cards presented on the following pages can be used in many ways to assist with the learning. When starting to work on the cards we assume that the child can 'hear' the first sounds of words, as when playing 'I Spy' (see page 36). Each letter sound is then learnt as the initial sound of a picture whose shape closely resembles the letter shape. Each child has his or her own set of letter cards and, as described on page 91, gradually builds up the pack of letter cards as they are learnt.

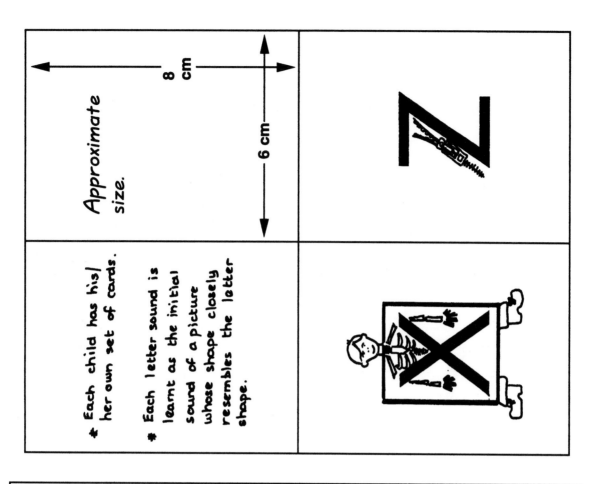

Approximate size.

8 cm

6 cm

* Each child has his/her own set of cards.

* Each letter sound is learnt as the initial sound of a picture whose shape closely resembles the letter shape.

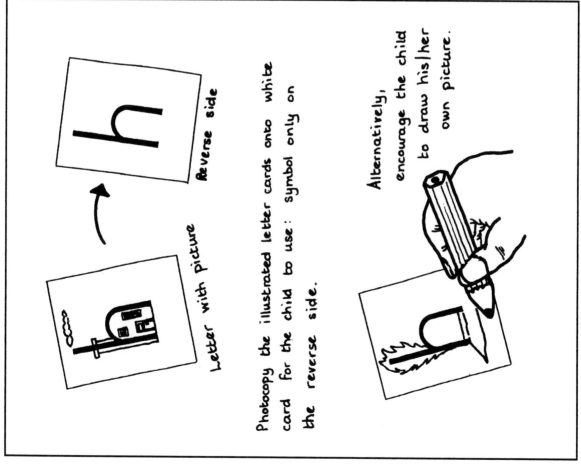

Letter with picture

Reverse side

Photocopy the illustrated letter cards onto white card for the child to use: symbol only on the reverse side.

Alternatively, encourage the child to draw his/her own picture.

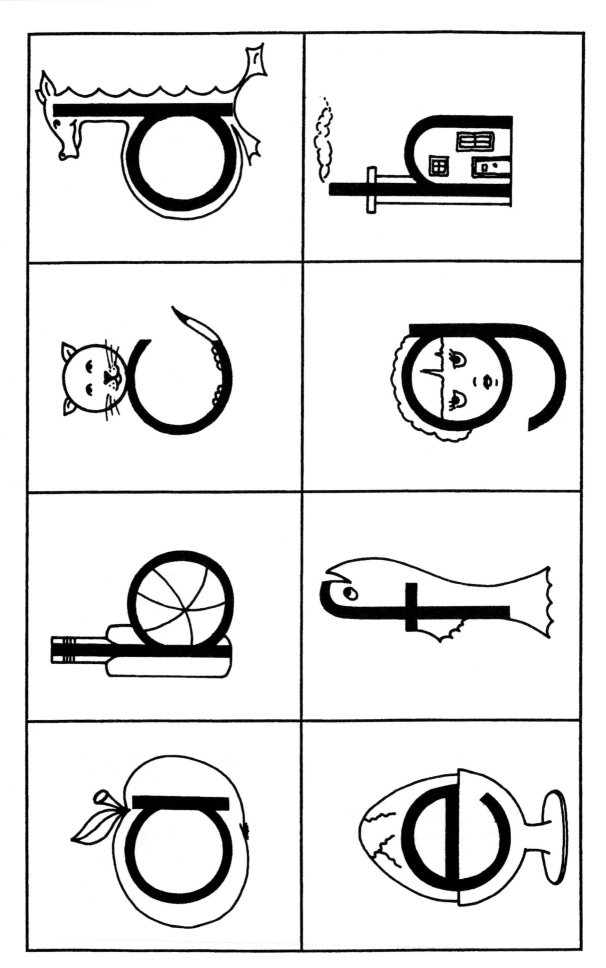

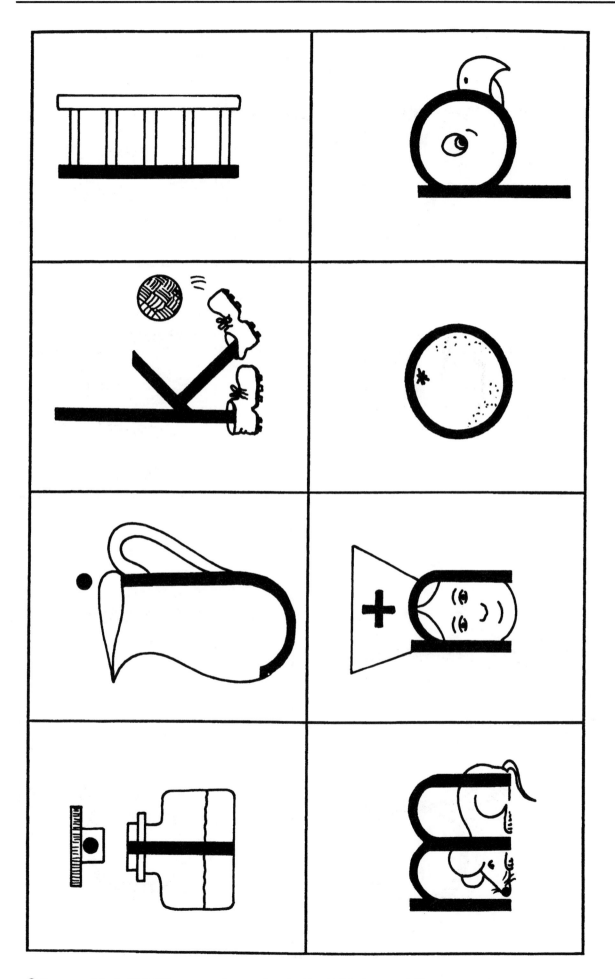

yellow

Chapter 7

PHONICS AT STAGES 3 AND 4

Teaching suggestions in this chapter help children learn the following phonic combinations:

Stage 3
- Consonant blends (e.g. fl, sm, tr)
- Consonant digraphs (ch, sh, th, ck)
- Vowel digraphs (e.g. ee, oo, ea, ai)
- Silent 'e' (e.g. cake, ride, rose, cube)

Stage 4
- Silent letters (e.g. write, knife)
- Longer word endings (e.g. picture, attention)
- Polysyllabic words (e.g. atmosphere)

N.B. Pages 125 to 129 provide further examples of the terminology used.

INTRODUCTION

On reaching Stage 3 children are usually well on their way towards learning to integrate contextual and phonological cues. Fluent readers absorb and apply phonics without necessarily being able to state them. They may learn, for example, that *ch* is pronounced *k* in 'chemist' because they have previously met the same combination in 'Christmas' and so few overt rules about these kinds of regularities need to be explained or memorised.

Our task is to identify and help those children who are not picking up phonic regularities so easily. We can determine the children's needs for more specific phonic practice by listening to their reading and examining their strategies when writing.

The learning of phonics is closely connected with the learning of spelling as described in Chapter 8. Poor spellers who have found the early stages of phonics difficult are likely to have a continued need to study words in phonic family groups. If children have marked difficulty with remembering phonic regularities, written 'multisensory' practice and dictation form an important part of instruction.

STAGE 3: BECOMING COMPETENT

The extract on the next page taken from Table 3.1 summarises the competencies which pupils will have acquired by the time they reach the *end* of Stage 3. It is included as a reminder that the purpose of learning is to search for meaning through language cues, phonics and fluent word recognition.

The three areas of **meaning, phonics** and **fluency** are considered interdependent in the learning process. If the child experiences difficulties in one area, other areas may to some extent provide compensatory strategies. For example, contextual cues can be particularly important in helping the child with phonic analysis.

We assume that children who are making steady progress will have reached a similar level in all three areas. Children whose phonic skills are weak, however, may have come to rely excessively on contextual guessing or on waiting for the teacher to supply the words they cannot read.

In contrast, those with better phonic skills sometimes continue to analyse and build up words which should have become part of their fluent sight vocabulary, and so their reading style remains slow and laborious. As much of written English does not fit easy phonic 'rules', it is important at this stage to encourage flexible guesswork. By following the teaching suggestions in Chapters 2, 4 and 5, other areas of reading are developed in parallel with phonic instruction.

1. Deciding what to teach

At Stage 3 children may have learnt many of the phonic regularities through analogy while reading and writing for meaning. The teacher's first task is to assess which letter combinations the pupil still needs to learn. This can be done in two ways. The first and preferred method involves listening to the child read and noting down errors and strategies. The advantage of this method is that it shows whether errors are phonically based or whether they are caused by other factors such as lack of understanding. **Chapter 3 page 45 describes and provided examples of a method of error (mis-cue) analysis.**

Stage 3: BECOMING COMPETENT

MEANING	PHONICS	FLUENCY
Uses context and more complex phonics to understand and predict meaning	Can read and write words with (a) consonant blends (b) consonant digraphs (c) vowel digraphs (d) silent 'e'	Extensive and increasing sight vocabulary from books read

---

A phonic checklist for stage 3

Checklists are the second way of identifying those letter combinations which still need to be learnt. Although this may seem an easier method, some specialist teachers now consider it to be too divorced from the 'real' reading process.

The checklists in Table 7.1 will help you assess which phonic structures have already been mastered. The lists are not all-inclusive; other checklists introduce letter combinations not mentioned here and vary the order in which the phonic rules are presented. You can make up your own checklists based on the phonic teaching materials available to you. **A selection of some common words is provided on pages 125 to 129 at the end of this chapter.**

Our subdivision of phonics into stages is also arbitrary in that there is no real cut-off point between Stages 2, 3 and 4. For example, words with the short medial vowel at Stage 2 (e.g. 'cat') lead easily to words with a short medial vowel at Stage 3 (e.g. 'spot') and more complex Stage 4 words draw on this information (e.g. spotlight).

The lists of words in Table 7.1, have been ordered roughly according to level of difficulty so that it is assumed that words from List A and List B are somewhat easier than the lists that follow. The words in the later lists build on the skills learnt earlier, for example, List D includes consonant blends and digraphs which should have been mastered at List A or B level.

Table 7.1 PHONIC CHECKLIST FOR STAGE 3

List A   Initial consonant blends: *br dr cl bl fr gr pr cl tr fl*
                                 gl pl sl sm sn sp sk sw tw

pram	glad	spot	step
trip	plot	skip	bring
blot	slip	crab	drip
clap	smell	swim	frog
flip	snap	twig	grass

List B   Final consonant blends: *ft nd ng lt lk mp nk nt sk st*
           Consonant digraphs: *ch sh th*

rest	lamp	shop	this
milk	hand	chip	rush
desk	ring	think	chest
lift	mint	ship	with
belt	sink	rich	wish

List C   Vowel digraphs: *ee, oo, ea, er, ou*
           Final consonant digraph *ck*

back	peel	week	keep
bread	boot	moon	food
sock	speak	team	meat
head	sister	winter	number
wood	loud	sound	shout

List D   Vowel digraphs: *ur, ow, ai, ay, ar, oa*
           Silent *e: i...e*

coat	stay	sail	mark
train	arm	start	crown
burn	burst	church	spray
down	wait	pay	soap
ride	shine	smile	cow

List E   Vowel digraphs: *aw, or, ew, ir*
           Silent *e: a...e o...e u...e*

draw	lawn	bird	first
gate	shake	stone	cube
fork	sport	tune	stew
game	straw	new	bone
short	shirt	rose	chew

The checklists in Table 7.1 can be used in the following ways:

(a)   Listen to the child reading. Write down words which cause difficulty and categorise them by referring to the checklist or the sample lists at the end of this chapter. You can use copies of Table 7.1 or the sample lists as the child's individual record form and check off the types of letter combinations he clearly copes with, while making a note of those which need further practice. Alternatively, you can design your own record form, if you find that Table 7.1 gives you insufficient space.

(b)   Use the words which illustrate each list as a test. Take List A as an example. Make up a set of cards by printing one of the words on each card. As the child reads the words, the cards can be placed in three piles: cards read with ease, those read correctly but slowly and those read incorrectly. If the child reads a word correctly but slowly, listen carefully to the strategy used in sounding out the word. It is essential that learners read blends and digraphs as one sound unit; if they sound out a word letter by letter, their strategy is faulty and they need to learn a better way. Write down what the child read when misreading a word. You may find, for example, that she read the initial consonant blend correctly but confuse the medial vowel. Use Table 7.1 as a record of the child's performance noting which words were read with ease, which were read slowly, therefore indicating a need for some more practice of that blend, and which misreadings demonstrate a need for more extensive help.

(c)   Alternatively, you can assume that if children can spell a word correctly, then they can also blend the sounds in it. Therefore, you might use the words in Table 7.1 as graded spelling tests to identify those children who have difficulties. This has the additional advantage of enabling you to screen the whole class at once if necessary.

2.   Teaching materials

Once you have identified the child's needs at Stage 3, appropriate materials, including games, can be obtained from a number of sources listed, for example, in the NASEN publication on phonic resources (see page 198). A selection of words to illustrate the phonic structures is provided at the end of this chapter. These are useful as a starting point for making up games such as Snap.

There is usually no need to repeat long lists of words to illustrate a particular 'rule'; a few sample words are sufficient. Ideally these words should be taken from the child's own reading materials so that we can encourage transfer to the reading of continuous text. For each phonic group to be learnt, select a word from the child's reading (e.g. **tree** for **ee**), and construct a short list of related words from the text (e.g. **see, sleep, week, need**).

3. Methods of teaching

(a)   For initial and final consonant blends and digraphs (Lists A, B and half of C) you can follow the procedure outlined in Stage 2 page 95 for word building. This involves adding plastic letters or letters written on small cards to the beginning or to the end of a medial vowel. As described in that section, you may choose either **Method A** (e.g. l-and, ch-at) or **Method B** (e.g. la-nd, cha-t).
Our illustration below follows **Method B:**

Final blends	Initial blends
la - nd	cha - t
la - sh	fla - t
la - mp	bra - t
la - st	tha - t
la - ck	sla - t
la - tch	spra - t

Make sure that blends are always pronounced as one unit. It may need several practice sessions with short lists of 'cue' words written on cards and, sometimes, 'clue' pictures (see below).

(b)   Initial cue practice in context: Initial consonant blends and digraphs can be learnt while reading continuous text. The teacher scans ahead, identifies an appropriate word towards the end of a sentence and covers up all but the initial blend and vowel of the word. The learner then sounds the blend and guesses the word from context.

(c)   A few children need more extensive practice using similar methods to those outlined under Stage 2 for single letter sounds. First, a picture cue is given, then a word cue, and finally the pupil is required to give an automatic response to the blend or digraph. For example:

Picture side   Reverse side

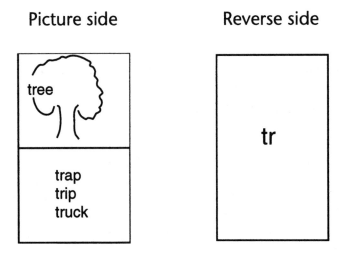

The child first names the picture and says the initial blend. She then reads the sample words underneath. After that she turns over the card and says the blend once more in isolation.

As at Stage 2, the child might like to choose his or her own picture cues and draw them. Introducing a few cards at a time, the 'quick flip' exercise (see page 93) is practised until recognition of the blends on the reverse side becomes automatic. The child eventually has her own set of cards with examples of those Stage 3 blends and vowel digraphs she has needed to learn. Even when the cards have been mastered, the child should go over them from time to time to ensure continued automatic recall. Older pupils may find it useful to carry a small, poc ket-sized learning pack of cards which they can produce for practice at odd moments.

(d)   Many children can manage without the picture cue and only need a few sample words taken, wherever possible, from their own reading. Each card in the set would look like this.

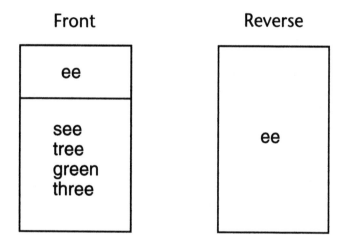

The child learns to read the front of the card quickly and easily. She then practises the recognition of the isolated blend on the reverse of the card using the 'quick flip' method (see page 93).

(e)   Dictation of words and sentences which illustrate the use of the letter combinations is recommended in conjunction with the drill based on the cards. For example, Hornsby and Shear (1980) suggest that, after the pupil has said the sound of the printed blend, he should be able to write the letters when the sound is said by the teacher. It is also fun to construct 'silly sentences' using as many words to be learnt as possible.

(f)   The best way to consolidate the learning of phonics is through reading and writing, where the child or the teacher notices relevant phonic cues and uses them as necessary. It is helpful to keep the set of cue cards at hand and refer to the appropriate card as to a dictionary. If the teacher can catch the child in the act of making use of recently acquired phonic knowledge, this is an occasion for congratulation, and an incentive for the child to look out for phonic cues in her reading.

STAGE 4: BASIC COMPETENCIES ACHIEVED

The teaching methods described for Stage 3 are also those followed at Stage 4. It is a matter of opinion as to how many of the more unusual and/or complex phonic structures should be taught. We prefer to teach the minimum, as we believe that pupils who have reached this stage can make good progress simply by reading and writing for information and content. The words causing difficulty can then become a starting point for further discussion and analysis. For these reasons we make no apology for excluding many phonic structures from the checklist in Table 7.2. If you think that a pupil continues to need a highly structured phonic approach even at this stage, you can consult, for example, *Alpha to Omega* (Hornsby and Shear, 1990) for more details.

Silent letters and longer word endings

The letter combinations represented by **List A** and **List B** in **Table 7.2** can be taught in a similar manner to those at Stage 3. A few words exemplifying each combination are written on cards and the pupil learns to read and write the set of cards fluently.

Compound words

Some pupils may not have learnt that many long words are made up of two short and relatively easy words. **List C** helps you to check this. Although compound words have been allocated to Stage 4, they should have been introduced incidentally at an earlier stage with examples such as 'bedroom', 'classroom', 'dustbin', 'dustpan'. Words taken from the context of meaningful reading make the best examples. When learning to read compound words, a few pupils may find it helpful to underline lightly each of the short words involved.

Polysyllabic words

List D gives some examples. In deciphering a polysyllabic word out of context, the pupil has to be able to look for manageable sound units, to merge these units and to guess the rest (e.g. wond-er-ful, cert-if-ic-ate, ex-plan-a-tion). For the purpose of

Table 7.2 PHONIC CHECKLIST FOR STAGE 4

List A Silent letters: *w k b h u c*

write	builder	scent	biscuit
knife	scissors	sword	scene
lamb	answer	knot	ghost
knee	bomb	guard	plumber
rhyme			

List B Longer word endings: *tion sion ture ous ious*

picture	furniture	adventure
attention	education	question
permission	discussion	impression
dangerous	marvellous	enormous
suspicious	unconscious	delicious

List C Compound words

cheesecake	rainbow	toothbrush	birthday
strawberry	roundabout	workshop	seatbelt
wallflower	lifeboat	anywhere	policemen
beetroot	doorstep	blackboard	sandpaper
countryside	peacock	handlebar	sunlight

List D Polysyllabic words

attractive	embroidery	telephone	confidence
impossible	atmosphere	photograph	introduce
automatic	surprise	completely	remember
wonderful	raspberry	explanation	develop
comfortable	certificate	economic	edition

practice it is helpful to attempt to underline the sound units first. It is obviously very contrived to learn unknown words out of their meaningful context and we prefer to teach such words as they are encountered during reading. In this way compound words and polysyllables are introduced quite early on, as soon as they appear in the books being read. Children can enjoy the challenge of trying to read and write such words, particularly as they find that the words are really only made up of quite easy elements, e.g. hipp-o-pot-am-us.

Long word jigsaws

Long word jigsaws are also a popular way of teaching polysyllables. Made according to the instructions below, they reinforce the skills of analysis. It is important to ensure that the child scans the words from left to right. Since the words are not cut into syllables, pieces cannot be lost or words confused.

(a)   Children make their own examples taken from their reading.

(b)   Use thin card, approximately 15cm x 7cm. Fold it longitudinally.

Fold

(c)   The word is written boldly on the lower half of the card. The syllables are marked lightly in pencil with the line extending to the top half of the card.

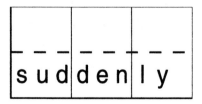

(d)   Cut through the top half of the card to make up flaps which cover each syllable.

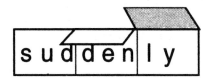

(e)   Syllables are revealed from left to right one at a time.

LEARNING PHONIC SKILLS IN CONTEXT

This method of teaching encourages children to use their phonic knowledge to check contextual guesses. By locating difficult words and working out strategies for reading them, the pupil is helped to take responsibility for the reading. The procedure is summarised below.

(a)   Let the child read the story or passage to you while you supply the unfamiliar words; the first 'read' is for content only without emphasis on phonics.

(b)   Talk about the content before starting word analysis.

(c)   Ask the child to find the difficult word, i.e. a word previously supplied by the teacher. Read the whole sentence again and pronounce the unknown word slowly and clearly.

(d)   Ask 'How could you have worked that out if I hadn't told you?' A good answer would refer to context and word structure, e.g. 'It must be "bridge" because it says "over the river" and it starts with br'

(e)   Say, 'How will you know this word next time you see it? Can you tell me how it is made?' 'Yes, br-i-dge.' 'Let's think of some more words with -dge.' Write them in the pupil's reading notebook:

> badge
> ledge
> fudge
> ridge
> judge
> wedge

'Read the words.' 'Where is the tricky bit?' 'See if you can cover up the words and write them as I say them.'

(f)   As the words have been entered in the pupil's reading notebook, they can be returned to regularly until the pupil can read and write them automatically.

(g)   A similar procedure is followed when teaching compound words and polysyllabic words.

(h)   Lists at the end of this chapter provide some words for each of the most commonly used phonic combinations. Select only a few sample words to illustrate the particular phonic structure.

RECORD KEEPING

Keeping records follows the principles already outlined in previous chapters and illustrated, for example, by Table 6.2 on page 99. The teacher specifies targets, or 'steps', sets a standard (e.g. a 'score') which indicates when the target has been learnt, and then makes checks at later dates to ensure that the skill or the knowledge has been retained. Include a heading for noting when a particular skill is applied in ordinary reading or writing activities and not only during lessons which the pupil knows relate to phonics.

To enhance motivation, it is important to involve the learner in the record keeping. A daily chart can be useful: the child gives a tick to those words or letter sounds read/written correctly and then gives the task a 'score' for the day (e.g. 12 out of 15). Always include enough mastered or nearly mastered items in the list so that the child can achieve a respectable 'score'. Further practice of those items which caused difficulty should then ensure that increasingly higher 'scores' are achieved on subsequent days.

SUMMARY

Our views and suggestions can be summarised through the following points:

• Teach phonics in parallel with enhanced opportunities for reading and writing as described in other chapters of this manual. Our aim is to foster easy and effortless reading, not over-reliance on word-by-word analysis of the text.

• There is usually no need to practise long lists of words which illustrate phonic structures. After learning a few words containing the particular structure the child is helped to apply the rule when reading or writing continuous text. We consider the teaching of complex or unusual rules a waste of time.

- Difficulties in remembering what sounds are represented by letter combinations can be reduced throught the use of mnemonic aids in the form of cue pictures or cue words provided in the manual.

- Reading and spelling are closely linked in learning phonics. In writing the child must attend closely to each element. When she can spell the relevant words without assistance we can feel confident that she has learnt the phonic structures involved.

- Children need to learn to isolate and blend phonic units so that they do not acquire the ineffective habit of attempting to 'read' a word letter by letter.

- Teach 'synthetic' phonics during frequent short sessions and ensure that each learning step is mastered. The learner should aim for speedy and automatic recognition of the words involved.

- Principles of active learning imply that repetition alone is not enough. Repeating passively a word 100 times without looking for strategies of memorising or self-testing is not likely to result in successful learning.

- Much of written English is not phonically regular. It is important to teach for diversity and encourage flexible use of all language cues.

- Tasks which involve memory are performed significantly better when the learner feels confident. It is essential that the pupil and the teacher share a sense of progress and, also, a sense of fun.

- Records of progress show what the child has learnt and which phonic regularities she is in the process of learning. When reading and writing with the child, teachers can provide appropriate prompts based on these records.

LISTS OF WORDS ILLUSTRATING THE MOST COMMON PHONIC REGULARITIES

The lists below are provided as a resource for teachers. They illustrate most common phonic regularities that may need to be taught more directly to those children experiencing difficulties with basic literacy. The lists only provide a limited selection of words. To reinforce the learning of particular regularities games such as Pelmanism may be made by writing the words to be learnt on cards.

Alternatively, teachers may wish to have the lists at hand when reading together with a child. As they come across a new word which is phonically regular, the lists enable teachers and children to look up quickly other similar words. For example, the word *count* may appear in the text. The teacher and the child may now choose two or three similar words, e.g. *out, house, mouth*. The words can then be entered into the child's phonic record book for repeated reading and spelling practice. They may be written on a card for the purposes of practice using the 'quick flip' (see pages 118 and 119).

Short vowels: *a, e, i, o, u*

at	pen	is	on	up
bat	ten	his	pot	cup
cat	hen	it	hot	pup
fat	red	bit	lot	cut
hat	fed	fit	cot	but
sat	bed	hit	dot	hut
mat	leg	pit	not	nut
rat	beg	sit	hop	Mum
bad	peg	wit	mop	hum
Dad	get	lid	pop	sum
mad	let	big	top	fun
had	net	fig	dog	bun
sad	pet	pig	fog	gun
jam	set	wig	log	run
can	wet	bin	cod	sun
man	met	pin	rod	bus
map	jet	tin	box	bug
bag	yet	win	fox	hug
rag		pip		mug
tap		zip		jug
map				rug
				put

Consonant digraphs: *ch, sh, th*
Final consonant digraph *ck*

chat	shed	that	back
chin	ship	than	kick
chip	shop	this	lick
chop	shut	them	lock
chimp	shift	with	lack
rich	ash	bath	luck
much	bash	moth	neck
such	cash	thin	pack
lunch	dash	thug	peck
punch	dish	thud	pick
bench	fish		pock
pinch	rash		rack
			ruck
			sack
			sick
			sock
			tick
			duck

Initial consonant blends:
bl, br, cl, cr, dr, fl, fr, gr, pl, sl, sc, sk, sm, sn, sp, st, sw, tr, tw

blob	drag	slab	spin
blot	drip	slam	spit
black	drop	slap	spot
block	drum	slim	speck
blush		slit	
	flag	slog	step
brick	flat	slug	stem
bring	flip	sling	stop
brush	flick	slash	stun
	fling		
clap	flash	scab	swim
clip	flesh	scan	swop
clot		scum	swing
club	frog		swish
clock	from	skid	
clash	frost	skin	trip
cling		skip	trap
	grab		track
crab	gran	smug	trick
crib	grid	smack	trust
crack	grip	smash	
crash			twin
crest	plan	snag	twig
crust	plum	snap	twist
	plug	snip	
	plus	snub	
		snack	

Selection of final consonant blends

and	ring	sink	belt	mask
hand	sing	link	felt	task
sand	thing	pink	melt	desk
land	wing	tank	kilt	dusk
band	song	rank		risk
	long	bunk	best	
end	singing		bust	tent
send	sailing	went	cast	sent
lend	ringing	dent	cost	rent
bend		sent	dust	
mend	camp	pant	fast	milk
	damp	hunt	fist	silk
bond	lamp			welk
fond	ramp	gift	soft	hulk
pond	limp	loft	lift	bulk
	bump	daft	gift	
	lump	raft	left	

Vowel digraphs: *ee, ai, oa, ou, ay, aw*

bee	rain	boat	out	day	saw
see	pain	coat	count	say	raw
week	fail	coal	our	pay	jaw
feet	rail	soap	hour	way	paw
meet	sail	road	mouth	may	law
keep	nail	goal	south	play	draw
seem	tail	boast	shout	stay	straw
feel	paid	toast	about	pray	prawn
heel	afraid	roast	cloud	crayon	crawl
free	plain	coach	proud	away	claw
tree	train	float	ground	display	dawn
sweet	brain	throat	aloud	holiday	yawn
green	chain	soaking	pound	today	hawk
sleep	again	groaning	sound	yesterday	lawn
sweep	snail	loaded	round		awful
cheek	complain	boastful	found		squawk
agree	strain		trousers		
between	entertain		thousand		
coffee	explain				
sheep					
teeth					

Magic/silent *e* with *a, i, o, u*

name	bike	nose	rule
game	like	rose	rude
came	time	hose	tune
cake	fine	home	use
make	wine	bone	fuse
take	line	hole	tube
bake	mine	pole	cube
sale	hide	mole	huge
date	rise	vole	duke
gate	side	joke	flute
hate	wide	vote	prune
save	pipe	note	excuse
wave	wipe	rope	
made	kite	hope	
safe	drive	code	
brave	slide	coke	
plate	smile	alone	
skate	shine	stone	
spade	white	close	
shape	slime	smoke	
snake	stripe	throne	
mistake	prize	explode	

Vowel digraph *ea* (as in *ea*t) or *ea* (as in h*ea*d)

eat	head
heat	lead
seat	dead
sea	bread
tea	tread
beat	sweat
meat	spread
neat	heavy
weak	ready
leak	steady
beak	health
team	healthy
bean	feather
meal	weather
speak	leather
steam	sweater
cream	instead
dream	
clean	
easy	
each	
teach	

Vowel digraphs *er, ir, ur*

butter	girl	burn
number	bird	turn
fern	dirt	hurt
term	firm	curl
under	first	fur
over	sir	purr
after	birth	turf
better	stir	surf
longer	skirt	spur
bigger	shirt	burst
faster	chirp	further
clever	whirl	church
dinner	dirty	murder
letter	thirsty	turkey
monster		burglar
summer		return
winter		

Vowel digraph *oo* (as in food) or *oo* (as in book)

food	book
moon	cook
fool	look
tool	foot
cool	soot
pool	hook
boot	good
zoo	wood
too	wool
soon	shook
roof	stood
room	blood
tooth	flood
shoot	crook
spoon	cooking
broom	looking

Vowel digraphs *ar, or, ew, au*

car	or	few
carpet	order	new
bar	for	chew
star	forget	grew
jar	torn	blew
far	torch	stew
bark	form	screw
mark	born	news
market	corn	jewel
harm	worn	crew
farm	fork	sewer
hard	cork	
dark	sport	autumn
park	short	sauce
card	storm	saucer
target	torch	author
garden	corner	fault
party	morning	automatic
art	record	
arm	inform	
chart	snoring	

Vowel digraphs *ow (as in owl)* or *ow* (as in slow)

owl	slow
how	low
now	row
brown	own
cow	grow
town	blow
down	flow
flower	snow
shower	show
allow	throw
however	window
clown	shadow
frown	pillow
crown	yellow
growl	follow
	elbow
	arrow

Part III

Spelling
and
Handwriting

Chapter 8

SPELLING

The learning of reading and spelling complement and support each other but need a different emphasis in teaching. This chapter covers the following areas of spelling:

- Selecting words to learn
- Planning help in spelling
- Developing personal strategies
- Regular and irregular words
- Learning to correct spelling
- The use of dictionaries and other aids
- Spelling games and activities

WHAT DO WE NEED TO TEACH?

Encouragement, enjoyment and understanding are as important in spelling as they are in reading. Encouragement and enjoyment come from success, and a feeling of being in control of the words. Children who feel in control of only a few words may limit their writing to what they think they can spell. Conversely, poor spellers who have something they urgently want to say may find that no-one can read it, not even themselves.

Against this background, the teacher's task is more complex than just to tell the child which spellings to learn. In this chapter we shall consider seven aspects of the teaching of spelling:

1. Deciding which words the child needs to learn next.
2. Planning help in spelling.
3. Helping the child to develop a personal strategy for learning spellings.
4. Teaching both regular words and less predictable words in such a way that they are retained.
5. Encouraging the child to take responsibility for making sure spellings are correct.
6. Helping the child to work towards independence in spelling by teaching the use of dictionaries and word lists.
7. Games and activities for learning spelling.

Chapter 9 examines clear and fluent handwriting as an essential element in learning to spell correctly.

DECIDING WHERE TO START

Deciding where to start teaching is the same in spelling as it is in reading: we look at the child's current work. This is easier in spelling, as we can quickly survey several pieces of independent writing, and decide what are the most pressing needs. It is important to have in mind a limited number of criteria here. It serves no positive purpose to note every spelling mistake in a piece of writing. This would in many cases give too much information, and make effective planning more difficult.

We have devised **Table 8.1** to help you to make planning decisions appropriate to the child's stage of development. By referring to it while examining the children's writing, you can decide what are their strengths, and what are their most immediate needs. You will observe that in many respects it is identical to Table 3.1, Stages in Learning to Read in Chapter 3. Because **Stage One** is concerned with the development of concepts rather than actual reading and writing, progress in both aspects usually runs hand-in-hand.

As for Table 3.1, the 'stages' include levels 1 to 3 of National Curriculum English. We have preferred to use the term 'stages' for two reasons. First, the 'stages' reflect our theoretical stance of how children learn to spell which is not identical with national requirements of what should be taught. Second, Stage One is much easier to achieve than Level 1.

TABLE 8.1: STAGES IN LEARNING TO SPELL

STAGE ONE
Recognises rhymes and rhyming words.
Blends spoken sounds into words.
Makes some representations of phonic structures in writing the beginnings of words.

STAGE TWO
Can write
- Single letter sounds;
- Words such as *at, in, hat, sun, dog, lid, net.*
- Some common harder words (e.g. *have, went, likes).*
Can analyse words into constituent sounds
(e.g. ch-ur-ch, re-mem-ber)

STAGE THREE
Can write words with:
- Consonant digraphs (e.g. ch, sh, th)
- Consonant blends (sl-, fr-, sk, -st, -nd etc)
- Vowel digraphs (ea, au, ow, etc)
- Magic e (came, mine, etc)
Spells most common words.

STAGE FOUR
Spells most words accurately. Knows when to use a dictionary.

N.B. We have preferred the term 'stages' to National Curriculum 'levels' as the 'stages' reflect our theoretical orientation and are not identical to the 'levels'.

Examples illustrating the 'stages'

Each of the examples is from the work of a child who is on the way to achieving the Stage specified.

Stage One
James has not yet understood th nature of sound-symbol correspondences. His writing is largely restricted to the letters of his name.

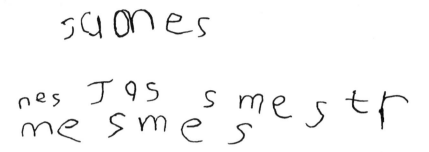

The fairy tripped and lost her shoe

Stage Two
Six months later, James is at the early phonic stage. He can write the prominent consonants in a word, and knows some common easy spellings.

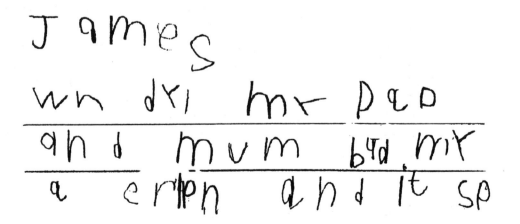

One day my dad and mum bought me an aeroplane and it snapped.

Stage Three

Yasmin knows many spelling rules, but sometimes over-generalises, e.g. *wighting* for *fighting; whachin* for *watching*

I don't Know why Im wrighting about politicsto me its all sphng imege and sterlg crisce but I have been dung my homework well if ive been bauyirog the Daily Start and whachin TVam but I have picked up some things.

Moving on from Stage One

Before the child grasps the principles of phonic synthesis at Stage Two, her attempts at spelling will probably be based on rudimentary phonic analysis. This may take one or more forms, for example;

- prominent consonants - **wz** (was), **Bt** (bought)
- letter *sounds* - **erpln** (*e-ruh-pl-en* makes aeroplane)
- letter *names* - **Is** (eyes), **nrg** (energy)

It becomes clear that, in order to prevent the development of spelling difficulties, children at these early stages need to be taught to spell the words they want to use in writing (see James at Stages One and Two above). They are unlikely to pick them up from their reading, or from copying under the teacher's scribing of their dictated sentences. They need to be familiar with syllables and vowels, and to develop techniques for learning spellings. And it is important to remember that a child may be at Stage One or Two in spelling not only in the Infant Department, but at the age of nine or ten, having made satisfactory progress in reading.
Games and activities for learning about syllables and vowels are to be found at the end of this chapter on page 148.

The importance of word analysis (Stage Two)

Spelling difficulties are compounded if the child does not 'hear' the component parts of a word. For learning to distinguish syllables, games of tapping out rhythms, or clapping each syllable in a name, are popular.
Further activities for learning syllables may be found at the end of this chapter on page 149.

The other important component parts of a word are consonant-strings. It is necessary to be able, for example, to analyse **spring** into **spr-ing,** to know the spelling of **ing,** and then further to analyse **spr** into **s-p-r.** This may require extensive practice.

PLANNING HELP IN SPELLING

To plan your teaching, look at one or more pieces of the child's writing with reference to Table 8.1. For example, Martin, aged 8, has written the piece below. We can see that Martin has achieved a few aspects of Stage Three, but is still unsure of all of Stage Two. We can list his strengths and needs in spelling.

'ALIEN'

Title given: Alien
Transcript
An Alien is scary
He has 6 eyes
and big teeth to eat
people up.
He has a friend
in space. He
lives in mud.
He likes talking.
His eyes flash
all the time. His eyes
are veiny.

an Alih iS SCry
he haS 6 eays
and dig th ee t o
eat pePle up
he haS a fehd
in Spac he
lives in med
he like ter King
his eays flesh
ul the thih. his easy
i re vea ney.

Strengths

Stage Two:
Knows most consonant and short vowel symbols; some short-vowel words (*his, in*);
Common words: knows *are, like*

Stage Three:
Knows some digraphs (sh, th) and blends (fl, sc)

Needs

Stage Two:
Revise oral word analysis
(t-ee-th, fr-ie-nd)
Consolidate all short vowel
sound – symbol correspondences.

Stage Three:
Extension of blends, digraphs, magic e
Common words: eyes, friend

Initial plan of action

Even from this brief analysis, there is enough evidence for weeks of spelling lessons, but the teacher has to decide on her first priority with Martin. Noting his spellings of **mud, flash,** she chooses to help him to consolidate the short vowel sounds. She does this by introducing the Medial Vowel game (page 149), which he can play not only with her, but with anyone who has already acquired this skill, including other children. Martin's difficulties with **eyes** and **friend** are common to many other children in the class, so the teacher decides to use these words for a 'five minute focus' with the whole class.

DEVELOPING A STRATEGY FOR LEARNING TO SPELL

A strategy for learning to spell is not usually acquired incidentally. It is safer to teach it. Traditional methods like copying out the word a set number of times, or spelling out in letter-names, are inefficient for some people. Most good spellers know when a word looks right, but some go by the feel of their hand writing the letters in sequence (the kinaesthetic approach). Others remember some rules, whether conventional or personal. Different combinations of approaches may be used by one person at different times.

In the past few years, since the publication of the first edition of this manual, many schools have adopted the Look-Cover-Write-Check routine, with mixed results. The biggest complaint is that children learn the drill, and then forget to make use of it when trying to copy or learn spellings. This is not surprising if children do not understand the purpose and value of the routine, and if it has not been practised sufficiently often to be automatic. It is best if children are helped to find their own most successful method of remembering spellings, which may well include some elements of Look-Cover-Write-Check. To do this, and to help those who find spelling exceptionally difficult, a Multisensory Approach is often advocated.

A Multisensory Approach

This means that the learner concentrates every possible faculty to imprint the spelling on his memory. It requires an act of will, and a belief that the effort is worthwhile. Because it seems laborious to learn at first, it is important that the teacher praises every small advance in acquiring the technique. It is helpful to the learner if the teacher explains :

"Let's try to learn this word in every way we can possibly think of. You can learn it with your ears, when you listen to yourself pronouncing the parts separately: with your voice, when you spell it out. Your hand can learn it when you write, and your eyes can be a camera to take a picture of it for your brain to remember. You can look for the bit of the word that tries to trick you, and make sure it doesn't. Let's see what your best way is of learning to spell." (Demonstrate each process.)

- Look at the word, read it, and pronounce it in syllables or other small bits (**re-mem-ber; sh-out**).
- Try to listen to yourself doing this.
- Still looking at it, spell it out in letter-names.
- Continue to look, and trace out the letters on the table with your finger as you spell it out again.
- Look at the word for any 'tricky bits'; for example, **gh** in **right.** (Different pupils find different parts of a word 'tricky'.)
- Try to get a picture of the word in your mind: take a photograph of it in your head!
- Copy the word, peeping at the end of each syllable or letter-string.
- Highlight the tricky bits in colour (or by some other means).
- Visualise the word again.
- Now cover it up and try to write it, spelling it out in letter-names.
- Does it look right?
- Check with the original.
- Are there some tricky bits you didn't spot (i.e. the parts that went wrong)?
- Repeat as much of the procedure as necessary to learn the word thoroughly.

This is an exceedingly lengthy routine. Encourage those who are having some success to slim the procedure down, so that they use only the parts relevant to themselves. This may take a little time to discover, but by thinking about the procedure, and experimenting to find out which parts are useful, pupils are more likely to develop a learning strategy suitable for themselves.

In the example quoted above, Martin reduces this fifteen-point procedure to six, and works out a routine of:

- **Look and Read**
- **Visualise**
- **Look again**
- **Cover**
- **Write (peep if necessary)**
- **Check**

He enjoys practising his spellings now that they have a personal challenge.
To do this, he takes a long strip of paper, half the width of an exercise page, and copies the word accurately at the top. After studying it by Look-Read- Visualise, he folds the word out of sight, and attempts to write it. Checking is done by unfolding the paper. At the end of several practices, the paper is folded over and over as in the game of consequences, with the word written on each section.

TEACHING REGULAR AND IRREGULAR WORDS

Choosing or adapting a spelling scheme

Many schools have adopted a published spelling scheme as an easy source of regular spellings. Children follow this at their own level, learning the weekly word lists and rules assigned to their group. The learning is often followed by a test. Make sure that the scheme you are using is suitable for your learners. Children who find spelling difficult need:

- words they are likely to find useful in their next pieces of writing.
- groupings that emphasise similarities in both sound and spelling, for example, **right, night, fight, sight,** but not **height** or **weight** until the others have been consolidated.
- both regular words in 'families', and less predictable but common words.
- opportunities to use the target words in context.

  Features of some schemes may contradict your own policy, for example:
- anagrams and crosswords emphasise constituent letters in a word, but do not encourage learning the letters in sequence.
- word searches should preferably run from left to right and from top to bottom, not backwards.
- in a scheme featuring joined script, the handwriting style may be incompatible with the school's chosen style.

The important thing is to be comfortable with any scheme you use, whether published or self-made. This may mean selecting and adapting to suit individuals, or the whole class. You may, for example, decide to ask some children to learn fewer spellings than the rest of the group, or enhance a sense of success by including in a child's list words that she already knows.

Testing spellings

Tests can give children an aim and a time limit and, if used supportively, can lead to a real sense of achievement. Of course, the ultimate test of success in learning to spell is when children have occasion to use the target word in spontaneous writing. It is disappointing to teacher and learner alike when, despite conscientious effort, the child fails to remember the spellings correctly in continuous writing or, worse, does not achieve full marks in the test. There are several ways of approaching this problem.

To test children on their individual spellings arrange for them to dictate the words to each other. The teacher can then spot-check progress or mark the tests. Children may enter the score on their own bar-charts and follow their weekly progress, without undesirable competition. Some children may learn five spellings, and some twenty, but they can all aim to achieve 100% of their target. With this kind of testing, the child and you can personally select the words to be learnt by any individual, with or without reference to a spelling scheme.

Dictating sentences

To give children practice in using their target words in context, many teachers dictate sentences with the words embedded. This gives the child a 'halfway house' between writing the word in isolation, and using it accurately in continuous writing. Many children, however, are slow to write sentences to dictation. They fail to remember the sentence, or have difficulty with handwriting, or cannot keep pace with the rest of the group. The teacher has to use her judgement to decide when a child will profit from writing dictated sentences, how many of the target words to include in one session, and how to organise the group of children.

Irregular words

Learning to spell cannot follow a completely phonic programme. Children need spellings right from the beginning that are either exceptions to general rules (e.g. **they, people**) or follow complex rules (**knew, brought**). It is advisable for children to learn these words as soon as they begin to make much use of them, since they will otherwise be in danger of consolidating wrong spellings.

Some teachers like to compose a list of commonly used words which they teach systematically, and have available to the children for quick reference. **Our own compilation of a basic spelling vocabulary appears at the end of this chapter on page 155.**

One problem with spelling schemes is that they must make assumptions about the words that children will want to spell, based on the child's age or reading level. This can be frustrating for a child like Martin who has an extensive vocabulary. If he wishes to write, for example, about a rocket **accelerating** into space, his teacher will supply the word, but it will not be at his level in the spelling scheme, and she may not have time to point out that **accept, access, accident** and **success** all follow the same rule. So although **accelerate** is not an irregular word, in this case it may have to be treated as one, and an opportunity to generalise is lost.

With truly irregular common words, such as **eyes** and **friend,** which all children need, and many learn to spell consistently wrong, Martin's teacher decided to highlight them with the whole class. She asked the children to consider the 'tricky bits', and invent ways of remembering the spellings.

No memorable ways of remembering **friend** were put forward, until the teacher suggested a sentence she had seen in a book:

"I fri ed my fri end on Fri day."

This appealed to the class's sense of the ridiculous, and was adopted immediately.

With **eyes,** the children devised a face as mnenomic. This was particularly successful, as it emphasised the symmetry of the word **eye** , the **y** forming the nose between the two **e**'s.

Where children persistently misspell the same word, or confuse reversible letters like b and d, they can be given a 'search card' as illustrated below. This is stored in a pocket inside the cover of the child's exercise book, or some other handy place. After finishing a piece of writing, the child turns detective, and searches every line to find any examples of these words which have managed to **misspell themselves.**

This approach makes correcting spelling into a game. It shifts the blame for the misspelling from the child to the word. It then becomes more acceptable to the child to try to control the 'unco-operative' word, rather than feel defeated yet again at having committed the same old misspelling.

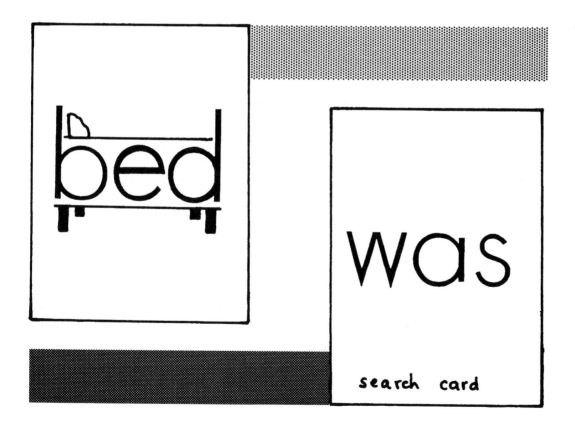

search card

TAKING RESPONSIBILITY FOR CHECKING OWN SPELLINGS

In an interactive classroom, spelling is not confined to studying the week's lesson on the appointed day. It is a topic that arises out of reading and writing throughout the week. If there is an odd five minutes to fill, the teacher may set the whole class to think of a word family, and find examples of it in books or their own writing. One Y3 class was asked to look out for words beginning with **some,** the teacher having in mind compound words like **something.** One girl got so carried away that she looked in the Little Oxford Dictionary, and found all the words, including **Somerset!**

Magic Lines

Teachers of children at early stages of spelling have found the use of Magic Lines helpful. When engrossed in the content of what they want to say, children are encouraged to draw a Magic Line to represent a word with a difficult spelling, and return to it later to write in the correct spelling. Below is an illustration of Laura's use of the Magic Line. It works better if the child can at least put down the initial sound. Some teachers have had to ration the number of Magic Lines per piece, as the writing otherwise becomes completely incomprehensible!

I am going to give my mummy a special and brilliant surprise and a diamond necklace.

Writing with the intended reader in mind

It is now generally acknowledged in schools that creative writing, as distinct from copying, is a messy process. The first draft is unlikely to be totally satisfactory. With each piece of writing, a decision has to be made about its purpose, and the intended audience. This will help to determine the standard of presentation necessary. For example, notes needed for future revision must be easy to read, but planning notes which will soon be scrapped do not need such care.

This situation is difficult for some people to accept. Fastidious children may hate to make mistakes, and will limit what they write to words they know. Their books are often smudged with eraser marks, and the idea of crossing out horrifies the child. Adults, too, may find the idea of a less-than-best presentation unacceptable.

But established authors feel free to cross out, scribble, cut, and rewrite. Writing is their medium, not their master. Children are interested to learn that Real Authors often scrap far more paper than they eventually send to the publisher in the finished typescript. It helps, too, if they see other children's work at various stages of development.

The teacher has to decide, with respect to each piece of writing, how much responsibility the child should take for checking and correcting the spellings, and which, if any, the teacher is going to correct herself. Her decision will be influenced by the child's competence in spelling, but also the interest the child can be encouraged to show in 'publishing' the writing for others to read.

A case example

Paying attention first to meaning, teachers comment on the content of the writing before going on to help children edit their work. The work of Ben has been chosen to illustrate how the child gradually takes over responsibility for checking and correcting the spellings. His progress has been monitored from the time he was eight. Ben has followed a systematic spelling programme for four years, and his spelling to dictation, although not perfect, is much improved.

Extract from a long story by Ben, aged 10.

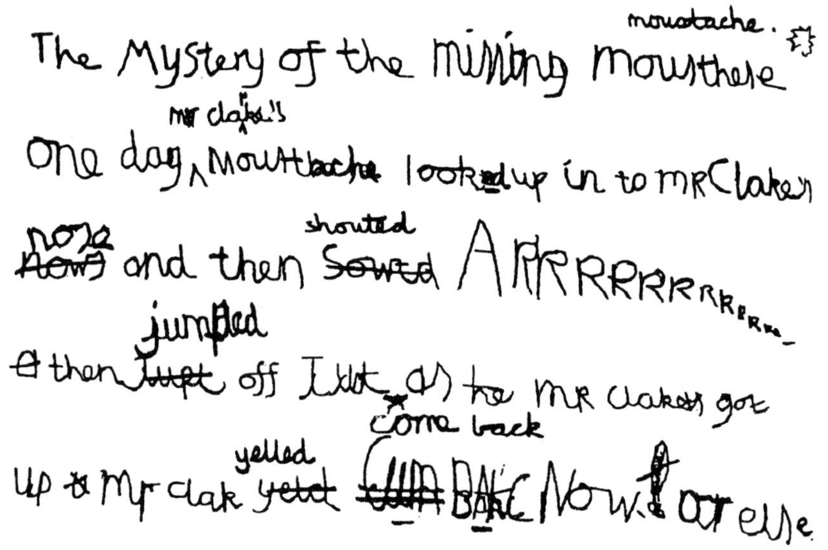

[Handwritten story, with teacher's corrections written above the child's words:]

moustache.

The Mystery of the missing mousthere

mr clake's

One day, mousthache lookedup in to mrClaker

nose   shouted

Hows and then sowed ARRRRRRRRR.

jumped

& then lept off I lit as he mr clakes got

come back

up to Mr clak yelled BAK Now I oo else

Teacher's comments:

"I'm sure Mr Clarke will be interested to read your story and find out what happened to his
moustache!...

One of your ways of spelling his name is correct. Can you tell me which
one it is? Perhaps you can find it written up somewhere in school.

Check the first five lines and make sure you have spelt
all your basic words correctly.

If you like, I will read through the rest of your writing and
put in the important words that people might not
understand."

(Teacher's Note: revise magic **e**, final **ed**.)

Extract from an even longer story by Ben, now aged 12:

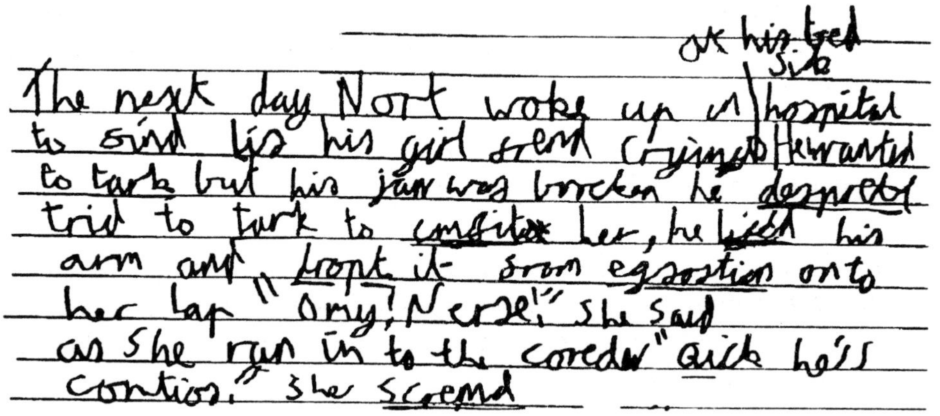

[Handwritten story:]

at his bed
side

The next day Nort woke up in hospital
to find lis his girl frend crying he wanted
to talk but his jaw was brocken he despretly
tried to talk to comfitox her, he liffed his
arm and took it from egsortion onto
her lap "O my! Nurse!" she said
as she run in to the coredor "quick he's
contios!" she screemd

Memore

..... The next day Nort woke up in hospital
to find Liz his girl frend crying at his bed side.
He wanted to <u>tark</u> but his jaw was brocken.
he <u>despretl</u> trid to <u>tark</u> to <u>cmfit</u> her. He <u>liftd</u> his
arm and <u>dropt</u> it from <u>egsostion</u> on to her lap.
"Oh my! Nerse!," she said.

Teacher's comments:
"This looks like an exciting story. Do you know how it is going to end?...
I see you have already started to check the spellings and underline the
ones that don't look right to you.
Read through the rest of your first draft.
Correct all the spellings you know to be wrong.
Put a line under the words you would like me to check, and I will tell
you which ones it's worth looking up in the ACE dictionary. I'll edit
the rest of it for you if you like, so that you can write up your
final draft neatly."

The teacher also notes word groups still needing teaching or revision. It will be observed that the tone of these comments is supportive to the child, and objective about the spellings. The teacher is not saying, 'You produce, and I will judge', but 'You have something worthwhile to say, and I will try to help you to make your meaning clearer'.

A PERSONALISED SPELLING PROGRAMME

The teacher's comments above show how it is possible to base the child's spelling tasks on the words he wants to use. To enable the child to classify words, and make the learning efficient, the teacher needs access to lists of words in the same spelling family. Phonic word lists for reading and spelling are to be found on page 125 at the end of Chapter 7.

Constructing individual word lists

Once the spelling rule or word family to be learnt has been decided, it is necessary to select words that are meaningful, and if possible, useful, to the individual child. For example, if the target word is **car**, the teacher could select **bar, far, star, hard, start** to be learnt in addition.

The obvious approach would be to give the child the list, and ask him to learn the words by his chosen method. Our experience shows that it is far more effective not to present the list to the child, but to get him to construct it, for example:

*"We are going to look at the word **car**, and other words in the same family. Let's say the word **car**, and listen to the sounds in it.*
*Yes, it goes **k-ah**.*
Now let's write it."
(Teacher spells out, child writes.)
*"The **k** sound is spelt **C**, and the **ah** sound is spelt **A-R**.*
*Underline the **ah** sound in **car**, and tell me the rule."*
*(AR spells the sound **ah**.)*
*"Now tell the sounds in **bar** (**b-ah**), and show me how you can write it."(etc).*

This approach gives you a quick check on how firmly the child has grasped the principle of spelling rules and families. We are in effect asking whether he can generalise from the rule to construct words he has not already seen.

The personal word book

A personal alphabetic word book helps children take responsibility for their own spelling. In it, they can put words from their own writing which are likely to prove useful in future. It is also a good source of words to learn, if children are invited to construct their own weekly spelling lists.

Where children know in advance what editing their writing is likely to receive, and their own probable share in it, they are often more willing to consult their personal spelling book, and any other word lists or dictionaries they can use easily. Easy reference is vital. Nobody wants to interrupt their flow of ideas by struggling with difficult reference books, or making numerous unsuccessful attempts to spell the word for themselves.

Tape recorders and wordprocessors

For the child who is unable to read her writing even immediately after the whole piece is finished, a small dictaphone may be useful. She can then periodically read into it her last sentence or line of writing, much as an adult writer constantly reviews what she has just written. The recording will be a help to both child and teacher in recalling what the writer meant.

The use of a wordprocessor, as described in the case example of Christopher on page 68, is of obvious assistance, particularly if it has a spellcheck facility. The Franklin Spellmaster, sold together with the Oxford Children's Dictionary, has proved to be another useful tool for helping children correct their spelling.

LEARNING TO USE WORD LISTS AND DICTIONARIES

Independence in spelling is achieved when the writer uses word lists and dictionaries successfully. The irony is that the writer must know enough about the beginning of a word to locate it in the dictionary, and poor spellers find this difficult. Picture dictionaries and topic-based word books are useful in the early stages, but their limitations are obvious. Many of the most difficult spellings are of words that cannot be illustrated.

Learning to use a dictionary requires more than a knowledge of the alphabet and the ability to put words in alphabetical order. There are many skills to be learnt, but these can be made enjoyable if they are incorporated into games.
The steps in learning how to use a word list or dictionary are set out below.

Learning to use a dictionary

The child can:
1. Recite the alphabet.
2. Read the names of all letters, and write the letter for each name.
3. Locate each initial letter in an alphabetic list quickly, looking for example towards the beginning for **D**, the end for **T** and the middle for **O**.
4. Quickly locate known words in a simple word list; for example, in the 500 Word Book, find **you, have, went, going.**
5. Put short lists of recognised words into alphabetical order, starting with easy lists with different initial letters.
6. Locate known words in a bigger dictionary.

Games for practising these skills are to be found on page 151 at the end of this chapter. Two useful publications for the early stages are Breakthrough *'My First Word Book'* (Longman), which lists very basic words, and has lines for writing the child's personal spellings, and the *500 Word Book* (Remedial Supply Co., Dixon Street, Wolverhampton WV2 2BX). This includes more words, and has space, but no lines, for the child's own words.

A spelling dictionary

The ability to use a dictionary to confirm a spelling depends on having at least some idea how the word starts. For children of ten or older who are still finding this difficult, the *ACE Dictionary* (LDA, Duke St., Wisbech, Cambs. PE13 2AE) may be useful. This lists spellings according to their initial consonant(s), number of syllables, and the sound of the first vowel.

The child needs to be able to analyse the sounds in words. If, for example, he wishes to write the word **gymnastics,** he must know that:

it has three syllables.
the first sound is **J.**
the first vowel sound is short **i.**

He would then be able to find **gymnastics** on the page of words beginning with the sounds **ji**, in the three syllable list. The procedure is laborious at first, but persistence pays off.

GAMES AND ACTIVITIES FOR LEARNING SPELLING

Once introduced, many of these activities can be supervised by other adults or children who have already firmly acquired the skill. All the games and activities for Phonics (Chapter 6 and 7) are relevant to spelling as well as to reading.

A set of small wooden letters, or letters printed on stout card, is needed for many of these games. Some teachers have found it helpful to paint the vowels red, to distinguish them from the consonants.

1. ANALYSING AND BLENDING THE SOUNDS IN WORDS

This is a spelling version of the word building game in Chapter 6 (page 95).

Procedure
1. Select a limited number of letters according to the words you are going to build. (For the example below, you need a, b, c, g, h, i, m, n, o, p, r, t, u) Check that the child knows all the sounds. If not, teach them with the flip-card alphabet (page 108).
2. The procedure is to make a three-letter word like *cat*, and by changing one letter at a time, make a succession of new three-letter words. Start by varying the first letter, and when you are sure that the child has mastered the process, switch to changing the final letter. Proceed to changing the medial vowel only when the child is fluent with consonant changes, for example:

I am making a word that I think you know. Can you tell me what it says?
Yes, cat. Which letters have I used for cat?
Yes, c-a-t (using sounds, not letter-names). Can you hear that cat is made of c-a-t?
Now I'm going to change the first letter to h, and that will make..?....Yes, hat.
Tell me the sounds in hat.
Show me how you can change it back to cat.
Now jumble up the letters, and see if you can make cat again.

Make changes as follows:

Change first letter	Change final letter	Change medial letter
cat	man	bag
hat	map	big
bat	mat	bog
rat	cat	bug
mat	cap	rug
	can	rig
	ban	rag etc.

2. THE MEDIAL VOWEL SOUND GAME

Materials
A set of the five vowels, either plastic letters, or written on cards:
A set of pictures illustrating one-syllable words, each with a medial vowel, for example:

> **cat, bag, hat, van, bat.**
> **bell, pen, bed, hen, net.**
> **pig, fish, zip, witch, pin.**
> **cot, dog, box, mop, frog.**
> **bun, cup, gun, nut, sun**

Pictures are provided on page 156

Procedure
> *Here are the vowels. Tell me the sound of each one.*
> *Vowels are very important, because each word has to have at least one.*
> *Let's look at the picture cards, and say what each one is.*
> *We are going to say the word for each picture card and put it in the column under the vowel we can hear in the middle. Let's see which vowel can win by getting five pictures first. So hen is made of h-e-n. It has e in the middle, so it goes in the e column. etc.*

3. LEARNING ABOUT SYLLABLES

At Stage One Reading, children learn to blend syllables spoken by the teacher into words. For spelling, they need to be able to analyse the words they want to write into syllables. Analysis of words into syllables is a more advanced skill than recognition of words pronounced in syllables by someone else. It may therefore require more preliminary work before the concept is grasped.

For syllables, collect a list of names from the class or school with varying numbers of syllables. It is not necessary at this stage to go into technical details about syllable boundaries. Start with a polysyllable, if possible the child's own name, or that of her friend. Show her how to count the parts or beats in the word, for example:

> **Mark/ Har/ri/son**
> **John/ Smith**
> **Va/nes/sa/ Bar/tu/lo/vic**

You can tap the rhythms on the table, or sing the syllables, giving a different note to each. The important thing is for the child to be able to separate syllables and count the beats for himself. Children need to learn the difference between vowels and consonants in connection with syllables, because every syllable must have at least one vowel.

4. THE NEWSPAPER GAME

The aim of this game is to raise awareness of grammatical usage and homophones, or difficult letter groups in common words, for example,

1.Grammatical Usage - where/were; there/their.
2. Question words beginning with wh - where, when, why, what, who, whether.

Materials
Sheets from newspapers or newspaper magazines, one for each child.
A highlighter pen or bright fibre tip for each child.

The game is best played in a group of two or three children.

Procedure
1. Decide on your target spelling combination.
2. Make sure that the news-sheets contain at least some examples of the target spellings!
3. Ask the children to highlight as many target examples as they can in a given time. You can give extra credit for reading the words in context at the end.
4. Players then check with each other that all the highlighted words conform to the set target. If you haven't time to discuss their findings with the children they can be asked to write two or three sentences using and spelling them correctly, either copying from the newspaper, or in their own words. The newspaper examples provide a model, so there must be no wrong usages or misspellings of target words.

The advantages of the game are:
- Children enjoy being 'detectives'.
- They see the words in context.
- They learn to use print as a resource for correct usage.
- The resources are easily available.

5. DICTIONARY GAMES

All the skills of learning to use a dictionary benefit from separate practice, away from the pressure of needing to find a particular word in the middle of writing a sentence. Once introduced, most of the games do not require teacher supervision.

As far as possible, materials for the games include the dictionaries and word lists in use in the classroom. This should prevent difficulties with transferring the skills from practice to the real situation.

6. ACTIVITY FOR ACCURATE LOCATION OF INITIAL LETTERS

Materials
Small lower case letters on card or of wood, one of each.

Procedure
1. Two children, or a child and an adult can play.
2. The child arranges the letters, in alphabetical order, in an arc on the table, so that each letter can easily be reached.
3. Each player takes it in turn to name a letter, which the other player has to touch as quickly as possible.

Variations
1. The player closes her eyes, and her partner tells her when she is 'warm' (close to the letter).
2. The partner says a word, not a letter, and the player must find the initial letter.

Extension
The game is played with a publication such as the *500 Word Book*, which has one page for each letter, and a thumb index for easy location.
It can be further extended by using a thicker dictionary in which to locate initial letters.

LOCATING KNOWN WORDS

Materials
A *500 Word Book* (Remedial Supply Company), or *My First Word Book* (Longman Breakthrough) for each participant.

Procedure
Each partner takes turns to ask the other to

1. Find the page with the word (e.g.*went*)
2. Find the word *(went)*

7. ALPHABETICAL ORDER ACTIVITY

It is easier to start with sets of words written on individual cards, so that they can be physically manipulated, before asking the child to work with a list of words on paper.

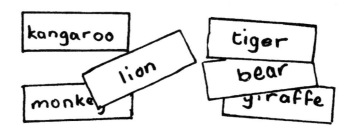

Materials
An alphabet for reference. Sets of words:

1. Initial letters in sequence (e.g. Carol, Brian, Anna,
   David -> Anna, Brian, Carol, David - A, B, C, D).
2. Initial letters all different, not in sequence,
   (e.g. plum, banana, orange, grapefruit, apple -> apple,
   banana, grapefruit, orange, plum - A, B,. . . G, . . . O, P).
3. Initial letters all the same., second letters
   different, (e.g. **skip, stop, save, send shout**).
4. A mixture.

Procedure
1. Place the cards in a column in alphabetical order, checking whether each one precedes or follows those already placed.
2. Where the initial letter is the same, cover it, and continue as in (1), arranging the cards in a column according to the second letter. (Initial S covered)

> kip
> top
> ave
> end
> hout

Some children may need to continue using this more concrete method of physically manipulating cards or slips of paper, before they manage to progress to the more abstract way of examining lists of words on paper. They can make their own cards or slips once they have grasped the principle of the activity.

8. LOCATING KNOWN WORDS IN A BIGGER DICTIONARY

Many children would benefit from practice in this skill. It has the advantage, once the procedures have been learnt, of not needing direct teacher supervision.

The teacher can introduce the game to large groups. When working without the teacher, two or three children can play together, taking it in turn to be the Question Master.

Materials
Identical dictionaries for each member of the group.
Pencil and paper.

Procedure
First make sure that everyone understands how to find the head words (target words). They are usually printed in bold characters.
The Question Master writes down a word for the players to locate. When playing in a group, the players write down the word and the page number. Those who locate it first help the rest to find the word. When only two players are involved, writing down is less necessary.

Progression
If the dictionary has 'catch-words' printed at the top of each page, indicating the first or first and last words on the page, these are a good starting point. Words near the top of the page, and in the first column of a double-column page, are easiest to find.

Variations
Find the first word beginning with ....
What word comes after ----?
Find the word beginning *ho...* meaning an animal you can ride on.
What page is it on?

9. THE READING-SPELLING GAME

This is played by an adult and a child, or two children reading the same book.

Materials
A set of alphabet letters.
A book that both children enjoy reading.

Procedure

1. Arrange the alphabet in a line across the table, with duplicate letters underneath:

```
        a b c d e f...
        a   c d e
        a       e
```

2. After reading two or more pages and discussing the content, the child

(i)   goes back and selects a word to spell (e.g. wanted);
(ii) reads the word in context;
(iii) using Look-Cover-Spell-Check, makes the word with the printed letters;
(iv) spells the word by letter-names, tracing the letters on the table with a forefinger.
(v)   when sure of the spelling, scrambles the letters, remakes the word, and checks with the word in context.
(vi) The partner checks the spelling, then attempts to spell it with the plastic letters herself.

The advantage of this game is that the child sets his or her own challenge. A surprising number of children select long and complex words, whether playing with a child or adult. The game gives practice in remembering letter-strings but it does not ensure that the word is retained for later spelling.

BASIC SPELLING VOCABULARY

A
about
across
after
afternoon
again
always
and
another
are
ask
auntie
away

B
baby
back
because
been
before
behind
best
birthday
bought
boy
bring
brother
brought
buy
by

C
called
came
can't
car
catch
children
Christmas
come
could

D
daddy
day
do
does
doesn't
don't
down
draw

E
each
eat
end
ever
every

F
family
far
father
find
finish
first
for
found
friend
from
front

G
game
gave
girl
give
go
goes
going
good
grandma

H
had
have
haven't
head
help
her
here
high
his
holiday
home
hospital
house
how

J
just

K
keep
kept
knew
know

L
ladies
lady
last
learn
left

like
little
live
look
looked
lost
love

M
made
make
many
may
me
minute
money
morning
mother
Mr
Mrs
Ms
much
mummy
must

N
name
near
never
new
next
nice
night
nobody
nothing
now
nowhere

O
o'clock
of
off
old
once
one
only
open
or
our
out
over
own

P
people
picture
place
play

played
please
police

Q
quick
quickly
quiet
quite

R
ready
right
round
running

S
said
same
saw
say
school
she
should
show
sister
so
soon
stay
stopped
stopping
street

T
take
taking
talk
teacher
television
than
thank
that
the
their
then
there
they
thing
think
this
those
thought
through
time
to
today

told
too
two

U
uncle
under
use
used
using

V
very

W
walk
walked
want
wanted
was
watch
watched
water
way
we
week
went
were
what
when
where
which
while
who
why
will
wished
wish
woman
women
won't
work
worked
would
wouldn't
write
writing

Y
year
yes
yesterday
you
your

Chapter 9

HANDWRITING

Handwriting as a skill supports the development of spelling. This chapter describes teaching and learning methods and materials. It provides suggestions for helping those children who have difficulty with the fine coordination involved in fluent writing.

INTRODUCTION

Handwriting is of special importance to children who find spelling difficult. People learn to spell by the 'feel' of the movement of their hand writing a word, or by visualising it written. If the hand has poor control, or forms the letters inefficiently or inconsistently, not only will the resulting appearance be unattractive, but accuracy in spelling suffers.

Handwriting is a craft, with a finite number of subskills to learn, unlike reading and spelling. Once a specific model has been mastered, refinements may be developed, but no further learning is necessary. But there are many opportunities for wrong learning on the way. Wrong learning is very hard to unlearn once the process of writing becomes automatic. The best way to ensure good handwriting is to learn it correctly from the beginning.

Since the publication of the first version of our manual, we have noticed a great improvement in the standard of letter-formation and presentation in children's handwriting. This is no doubt the result of the prominence given to handwriting in the National Curriculum.

Unfortunately, however, there will always remain some children who, despite well-structured teaching and dedicated practice, lack the fine motor control needed to produce neat, legible, joined handwriting. Such children need sympathy and understanding, and, above all, recognition of the effort they put into the presentation of their work, rather than objective assessment of the standard they achieve.

'GOOD' HANDWRITING

By 'good handwriting', we do not necessarily mean perfect conformity to a recognised model, or even compliance with strict standards of letter-formation and layout. We define good handwriting more broadly in terms of Legibility, Fluency, and Speed.

- **Legibility**: The writing is easy to read, not too small, with no ambiguous letters or spacing. Attention to learning to form letters and ligatures (joins) correctly can do much to help here.

- **Fluency:** This reflects how comfortable the writer feels with the model, and often indicates that handwriting has become automatic, with little conscious control. Fluency means writing in a flowing hand, smoothly and without obvious breaks within words or overlong pauses between words. Letter-forms may be adapted as the writer matures, but attention to letter-forms and ligatures is important when learning.

- **Speed:** A steady speed of writing, consistent with legibility, makes for fluency, and again suggests mastery of the skill.

It is clear that all these aspects of handwriting interact. Slow writing may produce a legible hand, but at the expense of fluency. Fast, fluent writing is at risk of being less legible. Children who are still learning letter-shapes will be neither fast nor fluent. As far as spelling is concerned, handwriting offers little support until it has become automatic. The child cannot easily pay attention to both letter-formation and letter-sequence at the same time.

For some children, improvement in handwriting is slow to appear because they have not fully grasped the necessary principles. It is helpful if these are taught directly, and referred to as reminders. If children are left to acquire them incidentally, they are just as likely to develop faulty concepts about handwriting.

CONCEPTS ABOUT HANDWRITING

1. Letters start at the top.
2. Letters have a 'body', which sits on the line.
3. All letters sit on the line, but some lower case letters
   have tails (descenders) which hang below:

g j p q y

4. Some letters have 'antennae' (ascenders) which rise
   above the body of the letter:

b d h k l

5. Capital letters stand on the line.
6. Some capital letters are the same shape as
   lower-case, but taller, and standing on the line:

C c   F f   J j   O o   P p   S s

LETTER SHAPES

If left to their own devices, children usually invent incorrect versions of letters, starting at the bottom instead of the top, and often going counter-clockwise round 'c- shaped' letters. In addition to concepts about handwriting, children therefore need to learn correct basic shapes. **These are shown in the whole page illustration on page 162.**

The principles of cursive handwriting vary according to the chosen model. They may be difficult for children to grasp, but it is as well if the teacher keeps them in mind when deciding how to help a child with handwriting:

1. In cursive writing, letters have ligatures which join them together.
2. Ligatures start at the end of a letter, as an 'exit stroke'.
3. Exit strokes may start from the top or the base of the letter. Depending on the style chosen, this may determine at what point the ligature joins the next letter.

paws   cows   comes

Note the top joins of o-m, o-w , w-s, and the bottom joins of a-w, e-s.

WHAT CAUSES CONCERN IN CHILDREN'S HANDWRITING?

Problems with legibility, fluency, and speed, and delay in developing the relevant concepts all lead to dissatisfaction on the part of both teacher and learner with the child's handwriting. For some children, additional difficulties are caused by lack of stamina, or poor muscular co-ordination. Left-handers may have additional problems. Careful observation of the child at work will reveal what it is that the child finds difficult, and may suggest some solutions. For example, if a left-handed child is seated to the right of a right-handed child, their arms controlling the pencils are in danger of nudging each other, and causing hostility as well as uncontrolled pencil strokes!

Handwriting style, whether good or poor, seems to become established very early in a child's school career. Maturation also plays an important part, so the teacher has the task of making sure that children are developing good habits, without making unreasonable demands on their stamina or co-ordinating abilities. To make the process as easy as possible for the child, it is as well to check the suitability of the following aspects:

- **Physical conditions**
- **Materials**
- **Chosen model of handwriting**
- **Teaching and learning methods**

PHYSICAL CONDITIONS

The foundations of good handwriting have been described as 'the three P's' - Posture, Paper-position, and Pencil-grip. These are all easy to check, but may not be so easy to maintain throughout a lesson. As in all aspects of handwriting, good habits should be established as early as possible.

Posture

To give children the chance to develop good handwriting, they should be seated at a comfortable height, with both feet on the floor, not on the chair spindle. Left-handed children may feel more in control with a seat that is higher than standard. There should be enough elbow-room, and left-handers should be on the left of right-handers. The non-writing hand should hold the paper steady, and brace the child in an upright position. Children who try to conceal their work from others by creating a barrier with their arms are not giving themselves the best conditions to write well.

Paper position

Children seem to acquire strong views about the 'proper' way to position their writing paper, but with a little flexibility, they can experiment to find the most comfortable position. For left-handed writers, this may be with the paper angled to the left and at a slight distance from the body, so that the pen can be pulled or drawn across the paper, instead of digging into it. Right-handers may also find it easier to angle the paper, but in their case to the right.

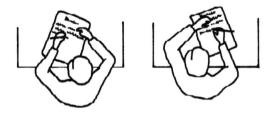

Pencil grip

This causes great concern among teachers, perhaps because so much has been made of 'correct pencil grip' in the literature about handwriting. The pencil should ideally be held between the thumb and forefinger, resting on the middle finger. For left-handers, they can more easily see what they have written if they hold the pencil higher up the shaft than a right-hander would.

A relaxed 'grip', if that is not a contradiction in terms, seems to be just as important as the correct position. Indeed, if the writer has difficulty changing from a less conventional grip, but is making progress in legibility, fluency, and speed, it is often easier to accept her preference, rather than cause stress by insisting on the 'correct' grip.

MATERIALS

Here we consider the writing materials available to the children, namely pencils, pens, and paper. A measure of choice in these materials can give a child a feeling of control over her writing, and the interest engendered is a help to motivation.

It is unfortunate when school or class policy dictates what kind of writing implement or paper ruling is available to each year-group. Children are not uniform in their needs at a given age, and uniformity of materials may have been imposed for convenience of administration rather than from consideration of what will help individual children to be successful. For the same reason, it may be as well not to attach too much significance to being 'grown-up' enough to use a ball point pen, or narrow ruled paper. It is preferable to stress what helps each child to present their work at its best.

Pens and pencils

It is conventional for Infants to use thick pencils, lower Juniors standard pencils, and older children 'pens' of various descriptions, whether fibre tips, ballpoints or fountain pens. This seems to work well for most children, but sometimes a few minutes' careful observation by the teacher will suggest that a different implement would enable the child to gain better control. Ball points are particularly hard to control for some people.

The condition of the writing point of the implement is also important. A blunt smudgy pencil, ragged felt-tip, or spluttering pen-nib make writing much harder for anyone, and give disappointing results to children who have put great efforts into their work.

It is a sad fact, however, that many of the children we have in mind find it difficult to organise their belongings, and often cannot find a pen, or try to make do with a broken stub of a pencil. It is worthwhile for the teacher to institute a system of checking writing implements in these cases so as to optimise the physical conditions for writing.

Paper and rulings

Infant children are usually offered unruled paper to write on, as they sometimes find it difficult to cope with lines in addition to all the other aspects of learning. They seem to benefit, however, if the teacher defines their writing space by ruling a line, perhaps halfway down the page. This gives them a box to write in. Some children, when they use ruled paper, continue to write in the 'boxes' between the lines In the example below, David writes under the line at the bottom of his picture.

In the list of Concepts about Handwriting, however, (page 159), it is clear that the line defines the relative positions of all letters. In handwriting lessons, therefore, practice in writing **on** the line is important even for young children.

Size of handwriting varies among children just as much as it does among adults, and it is this, coupled with personal preference, that should determine the rulings of the paper the child writes on. Large writing needs a wide ruling, but people with small writing also sometimes prefer a wide ruling. Offering the child a choice of rulings gives her another opportunity to exercise control over her writing, and take responsibility for its presentation. In the example below, this ruling is too narrow for Andrea's writing.

Andrea's writing is too big for this ruling.

Ready-prepared sheets, with printed borders, are popular with some teachers and children. These are usually unruled, and quite difficult to arrange the writing on. A line guide similar to those supplied with ordinary unruled writing pads, and securely fastened under the unruled sheet, can make a great difference to the finished appearance of the writing.

Daniel would have benefited from using a line guide

MODEL OF HANDWRITING

In the Handwriting Review, 1993, fifteen different handwriting schemes or systems are listed and described. Even when presented with such a wide choice, some schools prefer to design their own.

It is not our intention to recommend one scheme as superior to others in the present manual, but to bring to the attention of teachers the characteristics of styles which prove easier or more difficult for children with handwriting problems.

Print script or cursive style?

In response to the requirements of the National Curriculum, many schools are now teaching cursive (joined) handwriting in the Infant Department, some from Reception Class onwards. The results we have seen have been impressive, but cursive will not be the choice for initial handwriting instruction in all schools. Some teachers like to make a more explicit link between early writing and first reading texts, and therefore prefer print.

Choice of script scheme is important, and should take account of the subsequent cursive style. Most of the schemes discussed in the Handwriting Review clearly have the transition to cursive in mind, some to the extent of adding exit strokes to each letter.

Choosing a model for children with handwriting difficulties

Children with poor control or little stamina need a cursive model that makes minimum demands on their physical abilities. This means taking into account the general forward movement of the model, shape of ligatures, presence or absence of loops, and the shape of 'difficult' letters.

Models without forward movement generally look like print script with ligatures. The letters are rounded in shape, and stand upright on the line.

come   come

These characteristics seem to make it more difficult for the child to develop fluency and speed.

Ligatures are easier to control if they are pointed rather than rounded.

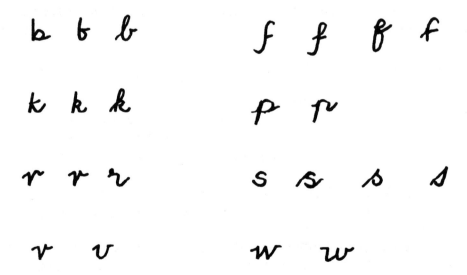

Pointed entry strokes also contribute to the general forward movement.

Loops, particularly ascending loops, are difficult to control. Their presence makes for continuity of line, and therefore in theory help the child to retain spellings by being able to continue writing a word without pause. In practice, effort may be diverted from remembering the spelling to forming the loops carefully, and keeping the pencil point on the paper.

'Difficult' letters are those which vary from one model to another:

It may be necessary to allow for some individual variation here, in order to enable the child to write without pausing to struggle with a difficult shape.

TEACHING AND LEARNING METHODS

How should we organise the teaching of handwriting?

The success of Infant children in learning cursive writing is probably due in no small part to their teachers' wish to prove the project valuable. This would lead them to very careful planning of organisation and methods, the key to which is small groups and close supervision. It is important for the teacher of handwriting at any level to be able to watch the children as they form the letters, to ensure that wrong forms are not accidentally acquired. This is easier with small numbers.

For children who have developed an inefficient individual style, it is often best to start again with a simple cursive model, not permitting the child to make use of the new style until it has become assimilated through supervised practice. There is no need for the teacher to do all the supervision. After instruction, parents, classroom assistants, or other adults can give the necessary practice and praise.

A useful resource for older children who are willing to practise at home is 'Handwriting: a Second Chance', a book of photocopiable worksheets by Philomena Pickard (LDA).

How can we promote legibility?

In teaching letters for handwriting, it is usual to group them by shape, not in alphabetical order. The procedure for teaching Handwriting follows a modified **Multisensory Approach** similar to that described for spelling. The teacher needs a writing board or sheet on which all the children can see clearly how she forms the letters. The writing of each letter is accompanied by a verbal description of the actions required. The children then repeat the verbal instructions while tracing the letter first in the air, and then on the table with a forefinger.They then write it on paper. This may be summarised as:

- **Read the letter**
- **Watch and describe**
- **Trace and describe**
- **Write and describe**

In order to practise ligatures and promote fluency, it is usual to write groups of the same letter together. Once a number of letters have been learnt, it is preferable to combine them in spelling strings and short words, rather than write groups of the same letter joined together, a practice which does not mirror the incidence of letter-groups in meaningful writing. It is convenient at this stage to combine handwriting with rehearsal of common difficult spellings, in order to make both letter-formation and spelling more automatic.

hhhh   www ooo eee yyy

how   now   when   why

The first line contains patterns that never occur in words.

How should children practise?

Many published handwriting schemes include work cards or other material for children to trace or copy. Tracing is not usually advisable for children with handwriting difficulties, as it encourages laborious 'drawing' of letter-shapes, rather than a rhythmic, fluent style. Copying should also be approached with caution.

There is no guarantee, when children are concentrating on reproducing the spellings and content of a piece of prose or poetry set as a handwriting exercise, that they are able to give sufficient attention to the accurate formation of the handwriting. Until they have learnt to form the handwriting shapes correctly and automatically, children's handwriting practice is probably better confined to very short exercises conducted under the supervision of an adult or another child.

How can we improve fluency?

Fluency is the result of automatic knowledge of letter-shape and ligatures, a relaxed hold on the pen, and rhythmic pressure on the paper. Knowledge of letters and ligatures comes from concentrated practice, as described in the section above. If the child is tense, and grips the pen too hard, or presses too firmly on the paper, rhythmic patterns with other media may help.

We suggest providing the child with plenty of cheap paper, for example newspaper or the back of wallpaper, and a thick paintbrush. Thinnish poster paint, or even water, can be used to get the rhythm going. The child should practise large, simple patterns with these materials.

Later, she can try producing the same patterns by finger-tracing on the table, then by writing on paper. By this process, we hope to refine control, starting with large arm movements, progressing to smaller wrist movements, and ending with finer hand movements.

The emphasis throughout should be on rhythm, not on perfect shape or even size. The child should be encouraged to think of the writing point as gliding or skating over the paper, not indenting it.

With children who have poor neuro-muscular co-ordination, fluency often improves if they are not required to maintain pencil point contact with the paper for the whole length of a word. It may help if the teacher discusses with the child the best places for her to insert 'natural breaks' in long words, perhaps after letters with tails, or at the end of syllables.

f ly ing fishes

How can we improve speed?

Speed improves naturally as the child's writing becomes more fluent. Practice of common letter-strings improve both speed and fluency. One teacher working with a very small group of children found that they were writing accurately but painfully slowly. He set them to write one line carefully and neatly, then the same line quickly and fluently, paying little attention to neatness. The children enjoyed having permission to be untidy, and speed improved over a period, without sacrifice of accuracy or neatness.

Lack of spaces between words

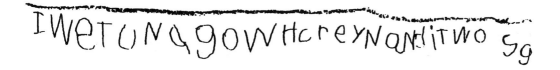

I went on a ghost train and it was scary

This problem may result from the child's difficulty with separating words in speech, but it is more likely to be caused by having too many aspects of writing to attend to at the same time. One solution often advocated is to encourage the child to use the little finger of the non-writing hand to measure the space between each pair of words. In practice, this means that the child cannot hold the paper with the flat of her hand in the approved way, and may find it difficult to see writing already done.

Making lists of words, as distinct from writing in lines, reminds children where the breaks come. It may be helpful to copy short lists of words into continuous lines, with the object of practising conventional spacing.

It often happens that when the child learns cursive writing, spaces between words are introduced without much conscious effort.

Reversed letters

It is usual for young children to confuse similar-shaped letters, whether reversals, inversions or reflections of the target letter. This becomes a problem when the child continues to be confused after most other children have learnt to recognise and reproduce the distinct shapes.

The difficulty can be prevented or resolved by drawing attention to differences in shape in both reading and writing, and by displaying a reference point or providing an individual reference card which shows a **d** for door, or a **b** for bookshelf or blackboard. By discussing the orientation of the pictures in the pictorial alphabet (pages 108 – 112), the teacher can help the child to get a mental picture of each letter. In handwriting, the letters belong to different 'families': **b** starts with a straight line, but **d** belongs to the family of letters starting with a c-shape. The letters need to be taught as members of these separated word families and not in close proximity to each other. Another way to remember **b** is to point out that lower-case **b** can be drawn inside capital **B**.

Capitals in the wrong place

Children use capital letters inappropriately for three main reasons:

1. They have not remembered which letters have tails below the line.

I had jelly at my Party

2. It is a safeguard against confusing reversible letters.

DaDDY caMe BacK

3. The lower case form of the letter differs from the capital form only in size.

My tech lets us Play FOOtball

The habit may persist even after the child has learned the correct forms. It helps if the child herself reads through her work to see if she can find perhaps three words where she has resisted the temptation to include her own 'favourite' capitals.

TAKING RESPONSIBILITY

Working towards improvement in handwriting is a matter for co-operation and negotiation between teacher and pupil. As in spelling or reading, the more the child takes responsibility for her own standards, the higher her achievements are likely to be. The teacher can help the child to take over responsibility gradually, by asking the child to check certain aspects of her own work.

For example, if **b/d** confusion is causing problems, the child can be given a check card (a small version of the reference card pinned to the bookcase), and asked to read through her work, giving a small tick to every correctly written **b** on a page. This is more positive than having the teacher mark all incorrect letters **b** and **d** wrong, and often leads to more care in writing.

Both adults and children are very ready to criticise their own handwriting as untidy or badly formed. This is not an attitude we wish to encourage, particularly in children who realise that they have other problems. By showing them how to look for what is good in their work, and sharing with them the responsibility for realistic improvement, we may hope to motivate children to persevere.

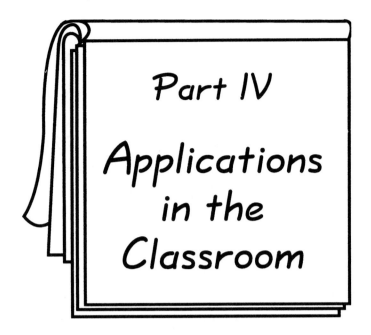

Part IV

Applications
in the
Classroom

INTRODUCTION

Descriptions of the practices of two classroom teachers provide a suitable conclusion to the manual. Chapter 10 follows the 'meaning - phonics - fluency' framework in planning additional help for a group of children. Chapter 11 demonstrates the pre-requisite classroom ethos and differentiation which enables children to become invaluable resources for each other.

We believe that the content of this manual is particularly suitable for the school-based stages of assessment and provision outlined in the Code of Practice on the Identification and Assessment of Special Educational Needs (Education Act 1993). Our main themes are summarised below.

- The three areas of meaning, phonics and fluency provide the basic framework for assessment and teaching.

- The 'stages' of reading and spelling development enable teachers to make approximate checks of children's needs. These checks are linked directly with the teaching suggestions offered in the manual. The 'stages' reflect National Curriculum levels but are not identical to them.

- The phrase 'interactive assessment and teaching' has illustrated the importance of fine-tuning initial impressions of children's learning in the light of their response to the teaching that has been planned for them. Plans are then adjusted to take account of these observations.

- The 'feel-good' factor, as an essential ingredient of success, has required constructive records, the children's involvement in their own learning and an ethos of partnership, particularly with parents.

Chapter 10

WORKING WITH A GROUP OF YEAR 2 CHILDREN

This chapter is based on the work undertaken by Bronach Bansal as part of the Diploma in the Advanced Study of Specific Learning Difficulties at Manchester University.

INTRODUCTION

This year I have been teaching Year 2 children in an inner-city school. On checking their progress I found that six of the children were still 'working towards level 1' in National Curriculum reading and writing. I decided to devise an intensive programme for them which could, as far as possible, be carried out with the group as a whole.

A record of each child's development and examples of their work are kept in a Busy Bee folder which follows the children through the school. Much of the information is in the form of 'records of achievement', where the children themselves are involved in planning and commenting on their work.

I examined the children's records and found some reasons for their slower progress such as frequent school transfers or illness. For two of the children English was a second language. All six were progressing quite well in other school work and their general language development was not causing serious concern.

I asked the school nurse to check again the children's sight, hearing and medical information to ensure that we had not missed any physical reasons for the slower progress in literacy.

INITIAL ASSESSMENTS

As part of the school's special needs policy, we have agreed some ways of providing cover for each other to facilitate small amounts of one-to-one work. I used this out-of-class time to check the reading development of each of the six children individually. I also needed to use some lunchtimes and breaks in order to complete the assessments quickly.

I read with each child and completed the checks described in Chapter 3 (pages 33 to 39). With some individual variations, the attainments of all six were quite similar and are summarised below:

MEANING

Stage 1 achieved: all can listen to and converse about stories. They understand most of the items in the vocabulary of reading and writing.
Stage 2 not achieved although the children expect stories read to them to make sense, and make good use of picture cues and illustrations.

PHONICS

Stage 1:
Rhymes: the children can nearly but not reliably complete this check.
Sound blending not achieved.
'I Spy' not achieved
Stage 2:
The children can give the sound for a few of the letters but I feel that they don't understand why they need to know this.

FLUENCY

Stage 1:
All children could match words and letters by sight and identify a few words by sight.
Stage 2 not achieved.

TEACHING PROGRAMME

Aims:

1. To develop phonics at Stage 1 through activities described in Chapter 6.
2. To develop the meaning aspects of literacy through the involvement of Year 6 children in reading with my class on the basis of the suggestions provided on page 27.
3. To build up fluency using a small number of words as described in the case example of William on page 71. (Because of limited teacher time, this was introduced during the fourth week of the programme.)

Week 1

(a) Developing knowledge of letter sounds

As none of the children had passed the 'I Spy' check, I played Easy Kim's Game (page 90) to help them acquire the necessary skills. The game was slotted in during the ten minutes leading up to morning assembly when children choose their own activities.

I assembled a tray of four objects each of which began with the same sound (saucer, spoon, sock, salt). Each child was asked to name the objects and I repeated the name emphasizing the first sound: sssaucer, sssock etc. The children repeated this.When all the objects had been named in this way I asked which sound they all started with. The procedure did not require to be repeated as they all readily grasped what I was doing.

I had a group of other objects some of which began with 'sss' and some which did not. The children examined these to determine whether they belonged to the 'sss tray'. They were totally successful with this activity. Finally, I covered the tray and each child had in turn to recall the objects.

This game was played on two consecutive days and on the third day it was played with the letter 'a'. It became part of the daily routine with each new letter taking about two days to be mastered.

In order to reinforce this work I began, from the first day of the programme, to play the 'I Spy' game when the entire class was sitting in the carpet area at storytime just before afternoon play. I used only the letter sounds that I had been practising with the small group. By the end of the week members of the group were putting their hands up to volunteer answers and accuracy levels were gratifying.

(b) Developing the meaning aspects of literacy

As I have a class of 31 children, opportunities for sustained individual teacher attention are spread very thinly. The teacher for the Year 6 Class and I decided to enlist the help of some of the Year 6 children. I chose 14 children from my class and included the six who were the focus of my intensive programme. We arranged to pair each of my 14 children with a fairly competent Year 6 reader.

A meeting was held with the Year 6 children involved. We gave them copies of the handout for parents (see page 27) and went over the points in it. We emphasised the importance of talking about the content and reading for the child if the text proved to be difficult.

The last ten minutes of the day was the most convenient time for both classes. At 3.05 p.m. each afternoon seven of my children went to their partners in the Year 6 classroom and seven from Year 6 came into my room.

Evaluation at the end of the first week: The Year 6 children seemed to derive a great deal of satisfaction from this work which made them feel 'adult' and responsible. I asked the group of six children receiving additional help how they thought the idea was working. They liked it. One boy said it was 'dead good' and proudly informed me that he had 'read' eight books that week. The positive attitude to books was evident in the whole group. At this stage I did not ask for feedback about the choice or content of books. They were enjoying themselves - that was enough.

Week 2

(a) Easy Kim's Game (page 90):
The letters 's' and 'a' having been mastered in the first week, I chose 'f' and 'l' for this week and repeated the procedure as described above. Reinforcement and revision was again undertaken at storytime with the whole class playing 'I Spy'. We now had objects beginning with a, s, f, l.

(b) Easy Clue Game (page 90):
As the children were developing a greater awareness of initial letter sounds I introduced this slightly harder game. I would say, 'It begins with sss and it is': a boy's name, a girl's name, an animal, in the sky, where you wash up in the kitchen etc. A different letter was used every day of the week and the game was fitted into a five minute slot just before the lunchtime organiser came to collect the children at midday.

(c) Daily shared reading with Year 6 as described above. The children continued to be enthusiastic about this.

Week 3

(a) Easy Kim's Game (page 90):
I chose the letter 'm' for this week and followed the procedure as in previous weeks.

(b) Easy Clue Game (page 90):
A different letter was chosen each day and the kinds of questions outlined above were continued.

(c) Consonant/vowel blends (page 95):
I borrowed a magnetic board and letters from the Nursery and put on it a selection of letters we had been working on: m, t, s, r, b. I checked the children's knowledge of these letter sounds individually: they had mastered them.

I now slid the letter 'a' down the list while the children repeated after me: 'mmma, ttta, sssa, rrra, bbba'. I found time for one such session daily. I enlisted the assistance of a parent helper who worked individually with those children who took longer to understand and learn this crucial step.

(d) Auditory sound blending (page 88):
Short sessions were carried out each day during the 'silent reading' period immediately after lunch. This work was undertaken initially on a one to one basis. To help with concentration, the child sat opposite me and looked carefully at my mouth as I said the segments of the words. As the children did not easily understand what was required, we tried clapping the sounds. Around this time I was also preparing class assembly on the topic of travel. I found a poem called Pony Trap Rap which the whole class was learning by heart. To reinforce this we brought out the percussion instruments and made a percussion sound for each syllable. By the end of the week the group had grasped the principle in an enjoyable though noisy manner.

(e) Daily shared reading
with Year 6 was continued. Their teacher was pleased to note the caring attitude of the children involved and the relationship that was developing between the pairs of children.

Evaluation at the end of three weeks:
I decided to examine the effectiveness of what I was doing. In the first week I had prepared a checklist to note the recognition and recall of letter sounds. I now repeated this check with each child individually. The children could recognise all of the consonants that I had taught them and also some that had not been directly taught or practised! They were less certain about the vowels e, o and u which had not yet been subjected to systematic practice. I also noticed that I had omitted rhyme awareness from the activities and decided to include this in my plans for the following weeks.

I read with each child in turn. I felt that the children were much more enthusiastic and willing to try to read for themselves. They sounded out the first letters correctly and, when I read words for them in syllabic chunks, they were able to blend the syllables and make up the appropriate words. It seemed to me that in tandem with the phonics, I now needed to start to develop their fluency with a sight vocabulary of commonly used words.

Week 4

(a) Consonant/vowel blends:
The magnetic board was again used and the consonants were those that I had identified through my evaluation as needing more attention. The vowel for blending with these was again a.

(b) Sight vocabulary:
I followed the suggestions provided under the case example of William (page 71). I chose 10 words from the book Icecream (a Sunshine reader). The children each made up their own Icecream Book through constructing sentences with the word cards and entering them into their books. We did no more than one or two at a time so as not to exhaust their stamina but also because that was all the time I had for it.

(c) Detection of rhymes:
This work was done with the whole class in the carpet area. We went through some nursery rhymes we knew and I explained the concept of rhyming. The rap we were learning for the class assembly ran to two pages and contained many examples of rhyming couplets. We also played Rhyming Riddles (page 88). I discovered that Year 1 had a set of commercially produced snap cards which I borrowed. I chose three of the fairly competent readers in my class and allocated two children from my group to each. I drew up a rota for the use of the cards so that each child in the group had a chance to play once a day.

(d) Daily shared reading with Year 6:
This was continued as before but I now felt that the Year 6 children might like a bit of variety and enjoy helping with the illustrated alphabet that I intended to introduce the next week.

Week 5

(a) Consonant/vowel blending:
A short time was allocated daily for practice with the magnetic board varying the consonants presented in front of 'a'. I wanted to ensure complete fluency with this task and continued to have the assistance of a parent with the two children in the group who were taking longer to understand and learn this.

(b) Sight vocabulary:
Sentence construction with the words chosen in Week 4 continued.

(c) Rhyme detection:
Working with the group I went through some more nursery rhymes supplying alternative words which were semantically equivalent yet non-rhyming, e.g. Ding dong bell, the Pussy's in the water; Jack and Jill went up the mountain; Ring-a-ring-a roses, a pocketful of flowers. The children then made up rhyming words such as hill, fill, pill. I was satisfied after four such sessions that this aspect of language had been learnt.

(d) The illustrated alphabet (page 108):
I made up six sets although I felt that four of the children were ready for letters without pictures. They were given the cards as emotional reinforcement rather than as an absolute learning necessity.

(e) Work with Year 6: On Monday afternoon when it was time for the children to disperse for shared reading I asked the Year 6 helpers to come to my classroom. I showed them the alphabet cards and gave them individual checklists of letters for each of the children. I explained the procedure of placing the cards, one at a time, picture side down on the table so that only the letter was visible. The children were to say the correct sound for each letter. If the children had any difficulty, they would be allowed a 'quick flip' to get the cue from the picture. I suggested a couple of minutes' work with the cards each day before the shared reading. After school I got some feedback from the Year 6 helpers. They said that the children knew more letters than I had entered on the lists so they had added two or three more.

Week 6

(a) Daily work with the illustrated alphabet and shared reading with the Year 6 helpers.
(b) Daily Rhyming Snap with partners as described earlier.
(c) Daily reinforcement of consonant/vowel blends on the magnetic board with the assistance of a parent in the classroom.
(d) Work on final consonants: I began the session with a dictation. I called out ten words and asked the group to write the first letter they could hear. The words I used were: biscuit, lemon, finger, zoo, pizza, mobilo, yellow, game, accident. All six children scored ten out of ten. I then revised the consonant/vowel blends using plastic letters and decided that the children were ready for a final consonant (see page 96 in the manual). I chose 't' and we blended as follows: ta-tat; ma-mat; pa-pat; ca-cat; fa-fat; sa-sat and so on. The initial consonant and vowel were always pronounced as one unit.
(e) Vowels and syllables: This was a whole class lesson. I told the children that every syllable had at least one vowel a, e, i, o, u and sometimes y. We examined a few words which we clapped out as syllables. For each one I drew a box on the flipchart.

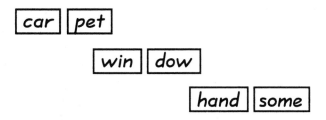

Then I asked for a volunteer to clap out the syllables in 'manager'. She clapped three so I drew three boxes. We looked at the first box which was to contain 'ma'. She got it right and completed the three boxes successfully. One of the boys in my special group also volunteered. I asked him to clap the syllables in 'tomato'. He clapped three times and whispered the sounds. I drew three boxes. He was able to write the syllables into the boxes. We were both delighted.

Weeks 7 to 13

The selection of activities continued along the same lines as in the first six weeks. Below I shall only mention new activities.

(a) Fluency:
New words were added to the sentence building from Mr Grump and, subsequently from other similar books. (level B Sunshine reader)
The children's self-made reading books gradually became more interesting as the vocabulary grew. Whenever possible, I would listen to the children re-read their own books.

(b) Book of the week phonics:
I borrowed four stories from Year 1 called Tog the dog, Mig the pig, Pat the cat and Zug the bug. I decided to use each one in turn as a special focus for the week.I began with 'Pat the cat' which I read to the whole class. It was excellent for reinforcing the words we had been learning which ended in 'at'. The children painted and drew pictures to illustrate the book and we made a display with the book as a centrepiece. The children in the group were encouraged to read and re-read the book either on their own or with a friend. Over the weeks similar activities were repeated with the other books.

(c) Magnetic board work with the series of initial consonants added to 'ig', 'og', 'ug':This was undertaken in parallel with the reading of the appropriate books mentioned in (b) above.

(d) Choral reading:
We had to learn songs for our production of The Gingerbread Man. I would sing a line at a time and the class would copy me. When every one was reasonably familiar with a song, I gave a photocopy of the song to each child. We read through the song slowly together pointing to each word as we went along. We practised the singing and reading once a day right up to the day of the performance. I think it reinforced the children's reading and memory skills.

EVALUATION

I decided to look again at the three central areas of Meaning, Phonics and Fluency to see how the programme was addressing these and with what effectiveness.

Meaning:
I felt that the shared reading with Year 6 was largely successful. The children were experiencing several books per day which would otherwise not have been possible. This activity was reinforcing concepts about print which in some cases were only tentatively grasped. But more important, the children were having

their imaginations and intellects nourished through a wide range of beautifully illustrated stories. There was a drawback in that I was not the person sharing the books with them and so could not check powers of prediction and comprehension. I did continue to read to the whole class at least once a day and used this time to elicit answers from the children in the group. I felt satisfied that their comprehension was on par with many of the other children in the class.

Phonics:

As much work on phonological awareness and phonics was being accommodated within the school day as was possible. Activities with the magnetic board, plastic letters and illustrated alphabet were a daily feature and were bearing fruit. Every child was responding to the repetitive practice though with varying rates of progress. Two of the children took a long time to grasp the concept of combining an initial consonant with its succeeding vowel (e.g. ma, ta, pa). In retrospect, the children might have found it easier to learn in the alternative way: h-at, p-at, s-at (see page 95). By now, however, all six had understood what was required and were attempting to decode when reading and writing for meaning.

Fluency:

We began with 10 words from the Icecream book (Sunshine readers). When the sound 'at' was introduced with the plastic letters and was combined with a variety of consonants, another 8 words were added to their accessible vocabulary for writing their own Icecream books: bat, fat, cat, hat, mat, pat, sat, sat. We did write some funny sentences! Over the weeks we moved on to the vocabulary of different books and added words from the phonics practice to our fluent sight vocabulary. By the end of the term the children had a good selection of words and a 'mastered and checked' sight vocabulary of some 30 words. They could also spell the phonologically regular words as shown by the illustration of Lee's spelling test below.

OVERALL EVALUATION

As I look at the checklists that I have kept, they show a rate of progress which I would not have dared to hope for when we started the programme. I now think that the children must have failed to grasp the beginnings of literacy at an earlier age and then become anxious and disillusioned about reading and, even more, writing. Over the weeks the children have regained their confidence, particularly during the shared reading sessions as their Year 6 mentors built up an excellent rapport with them.

For various reasons I chose to pair the children with the Year 6 pupils rather than involve their parents in the programme. But on parents' evening the father of one of the group said to me: 'My son was in school for two years and was at zero when he came to your class. You have taught him to read. We want to thank you very much.' I now think that I should probably have worked more closely with the children's parents.

With regard to the stages in Table 3.1, the children have completed Stage 2 for Meaning and Phonics and are pretty close to the notional 100 words under Fluency, if all the phonologically regular c-v-c words read with ease are included. Although I have encouraged writing in parallel with reading, I have not given priority to handwriting. I now wonder whether I should have, but there just was not enough time.

In terms of national curriculum reading and writing (even the harsher revised version currently under consultation) the children have now achieved Level 1. But this is only the beginning - they still have a long way to go. In terms of my programme, the children are ready to move on to:

- the suggestions in Chapter 7 for phonics
- the suggestions in Chapter 4 for fluency
- more direct attention to handwriting as described in Chapter 9
- continued opportunities for the enjoyment of the content of books as outlined in Chapter 2

In this account I have described an intensive programme for the six children involved. The programme has also had spin-offs for the other children. In particular, it has benefited those who were not included in the programme but also required revision of the earlier stages of literacy through the class activities that were introduced.

I have described the six children as if they were a homogeneous group. In fact, quite considerable differences are emerging. One girl is starting to race ahead of the others while two of the children consistently need more practice and revision in order to learn. I shall need to reconsider my groupings. Finding time for further differentiation will be even more difficult!

Finally, I want to emphasise that my work has been part of the school's identified development priority to examine how we notice and help those children struggling with literacy. As part of the school's overall policy, we now hope to be able to provide the continuity of help that the children need.

Chapter 11

CATCHING AND CONQUERING SPELLING IN YEAR 6

This chapter is based on the notes and records kept by Helen Moss. It describes the development of spelling practice in one primary school classroom.

INTRODUCTION

Much of the learning in my Year 6 classroom requires children to work collaboratively in groups. From the first day of a new school year, I start to develop a sense of community and the children's skills in working together. I structure tasks so that they require cooperation and involve every child. I start with simple activities, such as shared writing of cartoon captions, and gradually build up to lengthier assignments.

I tell the children: 'I am looking at how well you work together and not only at what you are making/doing. So how do you work together well? What do you need to do to be a good partner? What kind of person do you like to work with? I get answers such as 'they listen'; 'they don't boss me about'; 'they help me'; 'she says nice things about my work'; 'I'm good at ideas but ... is good at writing '(i.e. sharing skills). Given a choice the children want to work together. They particularly like paired activities.

At the end of the lesson we have a feedback session. Children describe the content of their task, what they have found out and then also the process of shared work : 'How did you feel when you did that work?' 'What was nice about doing this together?' 'How can we make it go even better?'

My most important strategy is to move about the classroom and tell children in a low key way that they are working well together. Even when I give more intensive attention to one group, I have to remember to show the other children at intervals that I am watching and approving the way they are working. Children must not think that cooperative activities have low priority when they are just left to get on with it.

I have found that when children work together they use each other as a resource. They develop a supportive and tolerant attitude towards each other. This gives me more time to assist groups or individuals with particular activities. But above all, I think that the quality of their work is improved. The children get inspiration from discussing the content of their writing or debating solutions to open-ended problems.

SPELLING

Despite these collaborative methods in other areas of the curriculum, the learning of spelling had remained something of a chore to be completed quickly so that we could get on with more exciting activities. On Monday mornings the children were given eight words to learn for that week. They had a formal spelling test on Fridays. Spelling practice was planned as a routine similar to 'brushing your teeth', to be done quietly without talking while I checked the register. The words to be learnt were usually taken from Charles Cripps's common letter strings (An Eye for Spelling, published by ESM). The children were split into two groups (Group A had eight children and were given words from the 7-9 age band; the rest of the class were in Group B and were given words from the 9-11 age band). Each child had an exercise book ruled with columns for the days of the week. After reading 'Choosing or adapting a spelling scheme' in Chapter 8 page 139, I noticed that:

- The children seemed to be spending more time staring out of the window than practising their spellings.

- Many children always got 8 out of 8 in the Friday spelling test. Did they need to learn these words in the first place? Or did the children spell the words correctly in lists for the test and then forget them?

- Four of the children in Group A, the lower spelling group, were struggling badly with the test. Although I was giving these children extra attention with reading and writing, their learning needs in spelling were not being met.

- Much teacher time was spent on dictating and marking the tests. Was this the most effective way of teaching? How could learning become more relevant and fun but not take up more time? Testing Spelling on page 139 in Chapter 8 gave me a starting point for rethinking my approach.

CHANGE OF SPELLING GROUPS

I looked at the children's written work in relation to the 'stages' outlined in Table 8.1 on page 133. The children were then divided into three groups based on these initial observations:

Group A:

Four children could spell single letter sounds, c-v-c words (e.g. **sun**) but seemed unsure of how to split words into their constituent 'chunks'. In terms of the 'stages' they needed to reinforce their learning at the end of Stage 2 and continue with regular words under Stage 3. Words to be learnt were now taken from an analysis of the common errors they made in their writing and then supplemented with a few similar items from my spelling lists. Words from the list of basic spelling vocabulary on page 155 were also included.

Group B:

12 children were near the end of Stage 3. Five of the words were now taken from lists of word families and three from their own writing. I continued to make up the lists for them.

Group C:

15 children spelt most words accurately, i.e. they were at the end of Stage 4. The children were shown how to select for themselves the 8 words to be learnt on the basis of errors that they spotted in their own writing. Each of them now had their own individual list.

NEW CLASSROOM ARRANGEMENTS

I decided to start the programme by teaching spelling for half an hour on the first Monday morning. I sat with Group A and demonstrated 'look-cover-write-check' using sheets of paper folded over as described in Chapter 8 page 138, or covering the word with a piece of card. Then I worked similarly with Group B and Group C showing Group C how to choose their own words from their writing. As the children practised this I moved from group to group and noticed that further reminders were needed of the 'look-cover-write-check' procedure as some children were still misusing the method.

The children were then asked to find a partner and work out ways for teaching each other spellings. They were encouraged to find strategies for remembering individual words through common letter patterns or syllabic 'chunks' and combine these with dictation and checking, in line with the 'multisensory approach' described in Chapter 8. Throughout the week there were opportunities for working with a partner. These activities were not teacher directed but could happen, for example, as the children came into the classroom in the morning. (Children can enter the classroom any time after 8.50 a.m. and do not need to wait outside.)

On Friday morning there was further paired practice for 20 minutes. First the children rehearsed their own word lists. Then their partner dictated their lists to them, marked them and entered scores in their individual spelling books. I noted that children usually achieved full scores, including the four children who had previously struggled with the spellings. There was no need for me to repeat the test. In any case, we now had individualised lists for Group C so that it would not have been possible. Instead I introduced the Spelling Mastermind game as described below.

Spelling Mastermind

The teacher is Magnus Magnusson and children are Contestants. He asks for volunteers who wish to be tested in their 'chosen subject', i.e. the eight words that they have learnt to spell. Having just practised the words with their partners, children feel quite confident and want to have a go. So the teacher chooses a volunteer: "This is Ms Smith and her chosen subject is...in what are you choosing to be tested?" The child hands over her list of words.

The teacher now dictates the words to the child who writes them on the blackboard. Teacher:"At the end of this test you have scored 8 out of 8 - a round of applause for Ms Smith." There are rarely any errors but if there are: "At the end of this test you have scored 6 out of 8; you passed on one item and one was not correct - a round of applause for Ms Smith." The teacher writes the correct version of the two words.

All the children wanted to be tested in their 'chosen subject' and felt 'lucky to be chosen'. Usually one child was selected from each spelling group. The 'scores' achieved were nearly always 8/8 but whatever the score, the candidate received 'a round of applause'. In later sessions children also took turns to act as Magnus Magnusson. The contest was completed with a brief discussion of the paired work. The children were asked: 'How well did we work together?' 'How can we make it easier to work together?' Answers now related more directly to the spelling task, with concrete descriptions of who did what and how, rather than blanket statements about sharing and caring.

EVALUATION AFTER THREE WEEKS

The changes had now become part of a new routine. My main observations are listed below.

- The better spellers were learning words they needed to learn rather than words from pre-designed lists which had seemed too easy.

- The four least able spellers also seemed to have more appropriate words to learn. The children had become confident with the learning routine. On several occasions I saw them voluntarily practising and checking their spellings with a partner . I continued to help them to devise strategies for remembering the spelling of particular words.

- The Mastermind experience resulted in many happy faces. The teaching partner was as excited as the child being tested, particularly as children of all levels of spelling did well.

- The 20 minute shared practice on Friday morning followed by Mastermind made spelling an exciting social activity. There was immediate and enjoyable feedback. It seemed much better than the previous solitary 5 minutes per day which had no direct link with the results.

- As the children had already checked and recorded each other's spellings before the Mastermind took place on Friday morning, there was no need for the old teacher directed spelling tests. My energy and time was spent on setting the task rather than marking it.

- It was essential that children recognised and appreciated progress at their own level. In discussing their achievements the children said: 'It's like aerobics - everyone at their own pace'.

ESSENTIAL ELEMENTS

- **Show children how to learn spellings through strategies such as 'look-cover-write-check'**

- **Differentiate the spelling task and ensure that the learner can succeed: "Did you beat your own score?"**

- **Teach spelling within a supportive social context.**

EVALUATING PROGRESS AFTER SIX WEEKS

Paired practice and checking

The children continue to seem at ease with the routine of paired practice. Previously, they spent much time staring about, keeping themselves quiet while the teacher completed the register. Now they seem 'on task'. Their attention span is longer and there is a buzz of interest. In retrospect, the solitary practice now seems like miserable drudgery. The paired testing also involves self-organisation and study skills - learning to use other people to help you to learn.

Choice of spelling partners

The spelling partner has to be someone at the children's table, preferably the person sitting next to them. Each table has even numbers of children. If someone is absent then the children can form a group of three and test each other. A supportive class atmosphere continues to be crucial. I am quite firm about rearranging groupings and partners for different purposes as I want all the children in the class to become friendly with each other and so avoid the development of cliques. When we come back after the half term holiday I intend to reconsider pairs and groupings.

Spelling Mastermind

David is the least competent speller in the class. This week it was David's birthday and he was chosen for Mastermind on Friday. He got 8/8. There was a huge round of applause and he grinned from ear to ear.

Methods of learning

I think that the children now understand what I mean when I say 'look at the word with intent'. All of them, including the four progressing slowly, look for familiar patterns and 'chunks'. David, one of the four, has started to take responsibility for his own learning. Take, for example, the spelling of **'light'**. First David said that it was too hard for him but then he worked with me on different 'ight' words and decided that he could do it.

It is important to supplement the spelling with other language activities, for example, a discussion of describing words (adjectives): 'a ghastly green gherkin'. We can then also consider the spelling of the words in these bizarre phrases.

Choice of words

At the end of last week I decided to check progress more carefully. I dictated the words to groups A and B who each had their own common spelling lists. Children in Group C had their individual lists so I sat with them and made some spot-checks of the words in their lists that week. I was satisfied that all the children could spell their designated words for that week. But I did not know whether words from previous weeks had been retained or whether the children spelt words learnt in lists correctly in their own writing. I decided to check this after the half-term holiday.

Examples of the kinds of words learnt each week are provided below. Note that I have not thought of building in revision from week to week and that the words in Group C (Simon's list is taken as an example) seem much more interesting than the words in the other two lists.

	Group A	Group B	Group C (Simon)
Week 4	fail	slave	sometimes
	tail	grave	fantastic
	nail	behave	shopping
	rail	haven't	register
	sail	gravel	particular
	snail	traveller	searched
	trail	loaves	syringe
	sailor	stopped	straight
Week 5	right	choir	merely
	small	chorus	stuttering
	shall	chose	certainly
	light	choose	silence
	hall	social	jolly
	finally	special	idiotic
	went	ancient	biscuit
	they	scientist	position

RETENTION OF WORDS LEARNT

Children had tested themselves only on the spellings that they had been practising during a particular week and with the words presented in lists. I had no measure of whether these words were retained or whether they were spelt correctly in their own written work. As it would have been too time consuming to check through their writing, I made up a story for each group containing a selection of 15 words that the children had been learning in the previous weeks. For Group C (own words) I selected words from two lists, Simon's and Rebecca's, which represented average progress within that group. I gave the three dictations immediately after the half-term holiday.

Group A dictation

One day Sally <u>went</u> to <u>feed</u> her pet dog Harry a <u>bone</u> but he had <u>gone.</u>
<u>Where</u> had he gone? <u>What</u> had Sally <u>done</u> to make Harry go off <u>alone</u>?
Sally <u>went</u> next door to ask them. <u>When</u> she went home, <u>there</u> was Harry.
The dog had got into the <u>house</u>. Sally was happy and Harry wagged his
<u>tail</u>. <u>They</u> were together <u>again</u>.
(The 15 words from spelling practice are marked)

Group C dictation (from Simon's and Rebecca's list)

To be a doctor of <u>medicine</u> it is <u>necessary</u> to read many books, learn how to
carry out <u>experiments</u> and <u>investigations</u> and <u>complete</u> many <u>exams</u>.
Working in a casualty department can be difficult. The <u>atmosphere</u> is tense
when the pressure is on. No matter how <u>awful</u> the condition of the patient,
it is <u>entirely</u> up to the doctor to stabilize the situation. <u>Sometimes</u> it is
necessary to <u>obtain</u> the <u>permission</u> of the relatives to operate. Doctors have
to take <u>particular</u> care at these times and <u>silence</u> is <u>certainly</u> needed.
(15 words)

Results

Group C achieved very pleasing results ranging from 14/15 to 9/15. This was
particularly remarkable because the words selected did not come from their
own lists except in the case of Simon and Rebecca (who both did very well). It
raised the whole issue of whether spelling was 'taught or caught' if you were
already a fluent reader.

Results for Group B were disappointing. Some children only got a few words
right and the highest score was 10/15. What was going wrong here? Had I
selected appropriate words? As I looked at my lists from previous weeks, I
noticed how uninspired the words for this group seemed to be in comparison
with the words chosen by Group C for themselves (see the examples above).

I was quite pleased with the progress of the four children in Group A who
needed extra help with literacy. Their scores ranged from 8/15 to 12/15. As I
had worked more closely with them, I now felt that they had indirectly
contributed to the choice of words to be learnt.

OVERALL IMPRESSIONS

Word families were easy to learn in lists but, out of the context of those lists, many
were contrived and bore little relation to the kinds of words that children wanted to
use in their writing. Children learnt the 'rule' for the test and got a high score, but
outside the test the words did not have relevance for them. I now felt that I should
extract only the most common 'families' and a few well known words to illustrate
them (as has been done for the phonic lists on page 125 of the manual).

Published lists did not provide any 'baseline' measures of the regularities that individual children needed to learn. Group A did quite well in the dictation. This may have been because the word families practised had been selected as examples of errors noted in their writing. It could also be that, used selectively, lists work better at the earlier stages of learning.

The words selected by Group C from their own writing looked exciting and relevant. I found it much easier to make up the dictation from the words selected by Simon and Rebecca than from the words taken from published lists for Group B.

The motivational effects of 'catching and conquering' own words seemed particularly important. But was spelling caught or taught? The majority of Group C children did well on words which had not been selected from their own lists. There were two possible explanations. First, although long, many of the words were not as difficult as they might first seem because they could easily be divided into syllabic chunks. Second, the children might already have known how to spell a good number of the words.

A REVISED SPELLING PROGRAMME

Choice of words to learn

Now all the children in the class are 'catching and conquering' their own words. The children in Groups A and B start the week by finding four words in their writing books which they wish to learn that week. I then sit with the groups and help each child in turn to think of four more words which exemplify the pattern of some of the words chosen. For example, if a child has chosen to learn the word **'measure'**, then she is helped to think of a second similar word such as **'treasure'** or **'pleasure'**. From the start children are involved more actively in the choice of words and in thinking for themselves of word patterns. Meanwhile, members of Group C are continuing to find all eight words for themselves.

Revision

Every third week children devise for themselves a revision list of eight words. They spot-check with the help of their partners previous lists in their personal spelling record books and decide which words merit extra practice. I monitor this activity closely and find time to sit with the four children in Group A to assist them with the choice and checking of words.

Practising spelling through sentence writing

As part of their spelling practice children make up 'silly' sentences or short stories based on the words listed in their personal spelling record books. They try to see how many words from a list can be fitted into one sentence or they have a 'contest' to see who can write the funniest account. From time to time we have class feedback where children read out their best efforts to the whole class. In pairs, children check their own spelling competence by dictating selected sentences, based on their own lists, to each other. I keep an eye on this to ensure that children do not end up practising any of the words in a misspelt form.

Spelling Mastermind

The Mastermind described earlier in this chapter worked well but gave only a few children the opportunity to become chosen 'contestants'. The new variant outlined below enables me to spot-check the progress of many more children in one session.

A Variant of Spelling Mastermind

As before, the teacher is Magnus Magnusson and the children are contestants. The Contestant comes up to the blackboard and hands over her list of eight words. Two of the words are now chosen at random from the list. Usually children get the full score of 2/2. If the child struggles, the teacher helps. The usual round of applause completes the turn. The game enables me to spot-check the progress of many more children quite quickly.

CHILDREN WITH SPECIAL NEEDS

None of the children in my class had very marked special needs. Even the four identified as requiring extra help were well on their way to literacy. I believe, however, that the classroom practices described in this chapter could have accommodated children with more serious difficulties. For me the three essential elements were:

- Children knew how to work together.

- They accepted that everyone makes progress at their own rate.

- They took responsibility for their own learning through 'catching and conquering' their own words to be learnt.

But there is much more to life at school than basic reading and spelling. The learning of spelling is one small aspect which must not take up too much time.

Children need to participate in all areas of the curriculum so that the stimulation of other subjects such as science or history can inspire literacy development.

POSTSCRIPT

I have now repeated the revised spelling programme with a mixed class of Year 4 and Year 5 children. I have made further adaptations to the programme to keep up the momentum of interest and to meet the needs of my new class. Many more of the children require the kind of help outlined for Group A above. I still think that it works well. Similar arrangements have been tried out by other teachers in the school and are now incorporated into our school's spelling policy.

BIBLIOGRAPHY

Adams, M.J. (1991) *Beginning to Read*. Cambridge Massachusetts: The MIT Press.

Alexander, R. (1992) *Policy and Practice in Primary Education*. London: Routledge.

Branston, P. and Provis, M. (1986) *Children and Parents Enjoying Reading*. London: Hodder and Stoughton.

Butkowsky, I.S. and Willows, D.M. (1980) Cognitive-motivational characteristics of children varying in reading ability: evidence of learned helplessness in poor readers. *Journal of Educational Psychology, 72 (3)*, 408-22.

*Centre for Language in Primary Education (1990) *Shared Reading and Shared Writing*. CLPE, Webber Row, London SE1 8QW

*Clay, M. (1979) *The Early Detection of Reading Difficulties: A Diagnostic Survey with Recovery Procedures*. Auckland: Heinemann.

*Clay, M.M. (1991) *Becoming Literate: the Construction of Inner Control*. London: Heinemann.

Cline, T. and Reason, R. (1993) Specific learning difficulties (dyslexia): Equal opportunities issues. Research section of *British Journal of Special Education, 20 (1)*, 30-34.

*Cline, T. and Frederickson, N. (1991) *Bilingual Pupils and the National Curriculum*. London: University College Educational Psychology Publications.

*Coles. M. (1992) Developing and extending the concept of apprenticeship: sharing reading in the classroom. In C. Harrison and M. Coles (eds) *The Reading for Real Handbook*. London: Routledge

Cooke, A. (1993) *Tackling Dyslexia: The Bangor Way*. London: Whurr.

France, L., Topping, K. and Revell, K. (1993) Parent-tutored cued spelling. *Support for Learning, 8* (1), 11 – 15.

Galton, M. and Williamson, J. (1992) *Groupwork in the Primary School*. London: Routledge.

Goswami, U. and Bryant, P. (1990) *Phonological Skills and Learning to Read*. Hove, East Sussex: Erlbaum.

*Great Britain, Department for Education (1989) *English in the National Curriculum* London: HMSO

Great Britain, Department for Education (1992) Curriculum organisation and classroom practice in primary schools: a discussion paper. London: HMSO.

*Great Britain, Department for Education (1993) *English for Ages 5 to 16.* Proposals of the Secretary of State for Education and the Secretary of State for Wales. London: HMSO.

*Great Britain, Department for Education (1994) *Code of Practice on the Identification and Assessment of Special Educational Needs.* London: HMSO

*Haring, N.G., Lovitt, T.C., Eaton, M.D., Hansen, C.L. (1978) *The Fourth R – Research in the Classroom.* Columbus, Ohio: Charles Merrill.

Harrison, C. and Coles, M. (eds) (1992) (Eds) *The Reading for Real Handbook.* London: Routledge

Hartas, C. and Moseley, D. (1993) Say that again, please: A scheme to boost reading skills using a computer with digitised speech. *Support for Learning, 8, 1,* 16-21.

Hornsby, B. and Shear, F. (1990) Alpha to Omega. London: Heinemann.

Johnson, G., Hill, B. and Tunstall, P. (1992) *Primary Records of Achievement.* London: Hodder and Stoughton.

Letterland (1993) *Picture Dictionary.* Letterland Ltd., Barton, Cambridge, CB3 7AY

Martin, A. (1989) *The Strugglers.* Milton Keynes: Open University Press.

Miles, T.R. and Miles, E. (1990) *Dyslexia: a hundred years on.* Milton Keynes: Open University Press.

Pearce, L. (1989) *Partners in Literacy.* Wisbech, Cambs: LDA

Peters, M. and Smith B. (1993) *Spelling in Context: Strategies for Teachers and Learners.* Windsor: NFER-Nelson.

Pumfrey, P.D. (1991) *Improving Reading in the Junior School.* London: Cassell.

*Pumfrey, P. and Reason, R. (1991) *Specific Learning Difficulties (Dyslexia): Challenges and Responses.* London: Routledge.

*Reason, R. (1986) Specific learning difficulties: the development and evaluation of an INSET manual on intervention. *Educational and Child Psychology, 3* (1), 45-58. Leicester: Division of Educational and Child Psychology of the British Psychological Society.

*****Reason, R.** (1990) Reconciling different approaches to intervention. In P.D. Pumfrey and C.D. Elliott (eds) *Children's Reading, Spelling and Writing Difficulties*. Lewes: Falmer Press.

Reason, R. (1991) Learning to cooperate and cooperating to learn. In *Developing Self-Discipline*. University College London: Educational Psychology Publications.

Reason, R. (1993) Primary special needs and National Curriculum assessment. In S. Wolfendale (ed) *Assessing Special Educational Needs*. London: Cassell.

Reason, R., Brown, B., Cole, M. and Gregory, M. (1988) Does the 'specific' in specific learning difficulties make a difference to the way we teach? *Support for Learning, 3* (4), 230-6.

Smith, B. (1994) *Through Writing to Reading*. London: Routledge.

Snowling, M. (1987) *Dyslexia: a Cognitive Developmental Perspective*. Oxford: Blackwell.

Stanovich, K.E. (1991) Discrepancy definitions of reading disability: has intelligence led us astray? *Reading Research Quarterly, 26* (1), 7-29.

Sterling, C.M. and Robson, C. (eds) (1992) *Psychology, Spelling and Education*. Clevedon, Avon: Multilingual Matters.

Stradling, R., Saunders, L. with Weston, P. (1991) *Differentiation in Action: A Whole School Approach to Raising Attainment*. London: HMSO.

Thomson, M.E. and Watkins, W. (1990) *Dyslexia: A Teaching Handbook*. London: Whurr.

*****Wallace, C.** (1986) *Learning to Read in a Multicultural Society*. Oxford: Pergamon Press.

*****Wasik, B.A. and Slavin, R.E.** (1993) Preventing early reading failure with one-to-one tutoring: A review of five programs. *Reading Research Quarterly, 28* (2), 179-200.

Watt, J.M. and Topping, K.J. (1993) Cued spelling: a comparative study of parent and peer tutoring. *Educational Psychology in Practice, 9*(2), 95 – 103.

*****Young, P. and Tyre, C.** (1983) *Dyslexia or Illiteracy? Realizing the right to Read*. Milton Keynes: Open University Press

* Referred to in the text

ADDRESSES

As it is beyond the scope of this manual to list or evaluate resources other than those included in the manual, the following two organisations can be contacted for comprehensive lists:

NASEN *
2 Lichfield Road
Stafford ST17 4JX
(0785 46872)

*National Association of Special Educational Needs

NASEN publications include:

- The NASEN A-Z: A Graded List of Reading Books (Hinson, M. and Gains C.W.)
- Phonics and Phonic Resources (Hinson, M. and Smith, P.)
- Games to Improve Reading Levels (McNicholas, J. and McEntree, J.)
- Assessing and Promoting Writing Skills (Alston, J)

Northwest SEMERC #
1 Broadbent Road
Watersheddings
Oldham OL1 4LB
(061 627 4469)

Special Education Micro-electronics Resource Centre

SEMERC publishes lists and evaluations of computer hardware and software and mounts exhibitions of the resources that are available.

INDEX